By Katel LeDû and
Lisa Maria Marquis

YOU SHOULD WRITE A BOOK

MORE FROM A BOOK APART

Responsible JavaScript
Jeremy Wagner

SEO for Everyone
Rebekah Baggs and Chris Corak

Design for Safety
Eva PenzeyMoog

Voice Content and Usability
Preston So

Better Onboarding
Krystal Higgins

Sustainable Web Design
Tom Greenwood

Design for Cognitive Bias
David Dylan Thomas

Cross-Cultural Design
Senongo Akpem

Expressive Design Systems
Yesenia Perez-Cruz

Resilient Management
Lara Hogan

Visit abookapart.com for our full list of titles.

Publisher: Jeffrey Zeldman
Designer: Jason Santa Maria
Executive director: Katel LeDû
Managing editor: Lisa Maria Marquis
Editors: Sally Kerrigan, Adaobi Obi Tulton, Susan Bond,
    Caren Litherland, Kumari Pacheco
Book producer: Ron Bilodeau

ISBN: 978-1-952616-13-6

A Book Apart
New York, New York
http://abookapart.com

10 9 8 7 6 5 4 3 2 1

TABLE OF CONTENTS

To the authors of the future.

FOREWORD

"I HAVE AN IDEA FOR A GREAT BOOK" is a phrase that a lot of people have uttered in their careers at some point. Unfortunately, not a lot of people get to bring that dream to reality for different reasons. I know this, because I've been there. When I first had an idea for a book, I didn't act on it for the longest time—I didn't think it would go anywhere. Many people—especially those in underrepresented demographics—feel the same way about publishing.

Ideas are a dime a dozen, but so much hard work goes into creating a book—from the planning stage, to writing, editing, and refining the content, to finally launching the book, either through a publisher or on your own. It takes a lot to turn a simple idea into a published book available to readers. But Katel and Lisa Maria have broken down the intricacies of this topic, and presented a clear and relatable path to publishing. I wish I'd had access to this content years ago when I was first beginning my own authoring journey.

Authoring is one of the most effective and exciting ways to share what we learn in our careers, especially as web professionals. This book will teach you the steps to take as you consider sharing your own insights, and help you gain the necessary self-confidence to get started. The sooner we start writing about our work, the sooner we can change the face of authorship in tech.

—**Adora Nwodo**

INTRODUCTION

"I THINK I'VE GOT AN IDEA FOR A BOOK."

We've heard these words uttered countless times by friends, colleagues, even strangers—and we love to hear them! But—they always follow up with a *but.*

"...but, I don't know, maybe my idea is only half-baked."
"...but, someone probably already wrote a book about this."
"...but, who even am I? I'm not famous."

The book you hold in your hands began with those very same words. Our idea wasn't fully formed; we're certainly not the first (or last) word on this subject; and, indeed...who even are we?

Well, for starters, we—Katel and Lisa Maria—are writers, editors, and publishers who know how to create thoughtful, professional books that people want to read. We have decades of experience speaking, teaching, consulting, and coaching in the tech industry and beyond. And we believe the process of pitching, drafting, editing, publishing, and selling books—particularly in the tech space—should involve humility and humanity. It should open more doors, and for more people, than it closes.

That said, we want to acknowledge our blind spots, too: we are both college-educated, able-bodied, cis white American women whose direct book-publishing expertise derives mostly from a single organization: A Book Apart. While we hope our perspective is useful, it is also bound to be limited in certain respects.

Although this book mainly covers writing about technical and professional subjects, we hope our guidance will help you pursue book-writing regardless of your topic, background, or publishing goals. We speak to the way we do things at A Book Apart, but with an eye toward alternatives, such as approaching other publishers or self-publishing.

Whether you've got a tiny spark of a book idea, a fully realized manuscript looking for its forever home, or something in that complex space in between, we want you to know that you've already got us in your corner. We want to support your writing quest, whatever that may look like. No matter your writing style, experience level, or career path, we share a common goal: one day, you *should* write and publish a book. Because the more people speak up and share their perspectives, the better the web industry—and everyone's work in it—becomes.

In our time at A Book Apart, we've been privileged to work with dozens of authors on their writing processes. We know that every author has a unique voice, and we strive to bring out the best in each. We know how to pull seemingly disparate ideas together to build a cohesive narrative, and we know how to relay that narrative so that it reaches its intended audience—and lands. We know, it seems, a thing or two about publishing books—by web workers, for web workers.

Turns out that writing a book was within our reach. And it's absolutely within yours, too.

THE TRUTH ABOUT PUBLISHING

> *If you are going to be a writer, there is nothing I can say to stop you; if you're not going to be a writer, nothing I can say will help you. What you really need at the beginning is somebody to let you know that the effort is real.*
> —JAMES BALDWIN

DECIDING THAT YOU WANT to write a book feels risky. Making that call means making a commitment to your ideas—and to the considerable work of translating those ideas to the page. It's an act of vulnerability, public in a way that many other career ventures are not. You are, in essence, declaring an intention to take up space—and society doesn't always support folks in that endeavor.

People who "write books" have, historically, looked an awful lot like people who hold the most societal power: middle- and upper-class, formally educated, white, and male. Those people, in turn, have granted value to the idea of *being published*, earned or not. Over the centuries, this insidious loop has worked to reserve authorship for a homogenous few, frequently keeping it out of reach for writers with marginalized identities.

While publishing today is more democratic *on paper*—helped by the internet, self-publishing solutions, and the continued labor of activists and unions—there's no shortage of obstacles that silence would-be authors. Institutional oppression, professional insecurities, and even your own fears can keep the fires of self-doubt burning, convincing you to abandon or put off (indefinitely!) your publishing dreams.

We are confident that if you *want* to write a book, you *can* write a book—and that starts with naming the obstacles ahead so you'll be better equipped to clear them.

HOW PUBLISHING STARTED

The history of printing and publishing is itself typically whitewashed. *Quelle surprise;* we know. We won't give you a (long) history lesson here, but we do want to reflect on what publishing's past has imprinted on its present (pun intended).

Writing first came about during the Bronze Age, independently arising in China, Egypt, Mesopotamia, and Mesoamerica (http://bkaprt.com/ysw40/01-01/). Writing and reproduction work was usually performed by a scribe, which in many cultures became an elevated position in society (http://bkaprt.com/ysw40/01-02/). For thousands of years, publishing was manual, painstaking, and extremely time-consuming to produce, which made written reproductions very expensive to own, and limited literacy to the elite.

Printing with blocks of wood, clay, stone, and metal is also an ancient practice, but it's the invention of movable type that really kicked off the concept of publishing. Bi Sheng first created movable type in China during the 1040s (http://bkaprt.com/ysw40/01-03/), and Johannes Gutenberg created Europe's first movable type printing press somewhere between the late 1430s and early 1450s (http://bkaprt.com/ysw40/01-04/). Gutenberg's printing press marked a turning point in widespread access to the written word—and an accompanying rise in literacy—in the West. Publishing progressed hand in hand with the development of literature, bureaucracy, propaganda, and written works of all lengths, styles, and genres.

But while publishing brought the written word to many more people, it didn't exactly level the playing field with regard to access and authorship. The people with the power to print books—that is, with the money to fund printing presses and the clout to support authors—were the same as they'd always been: usually wealthy, white, and male.

DEMOCRATIZING THE INDUSTRY

The landscape shifted slightly in 1979 when Dan Poynter wrote and published *The Self-Publishing Manual* (http://bkaprt.com/ysw40/01-05/). Poynter was an author, publisher, speaker, and enthusiastic parachutist and skydiver. We know—we weren't certain that tidbit was relevant either, but it is: Poynter started his career designing parachutes and wrote prolifically about their design and use. When he became interested in hang gliding and couldn't find a book about it, he wrote his own—which led him to writing about self-publishing and founding a publishing company (http://bkaprt.com/ysw40/01-06/).

Self-publishing opened up an enormous opportunity for authors of any skill level, in any genre, with any size audience, to share their ideas and voices with the world. Many authors jumped eagerly into self-publishing in the 1980s and 1990s, printing consignment runs and selling their books by mail order, or driving around to bookshops with fresh-off-the-press books loaded into their cars. Print-on-demand capabilities and availability grew, and in 1990 the ebook was born—though it was still unwieldy to sell books directly to readers. It wasn't until 1998 that selling books online became more ubiquitous (http://bkaprt.com/ysw40/01-07/).

Then along came Amazon, and everything changed monumentally. Their publishing services and distribution structure made self-publishing incredibly approachable—literally anyone could now publish *and sell* a book. And folks have been doing so with wild abandon ever since—which, from an access and equality perspective, is honestly pretty cool.

But that ease and efficiency often come at the cost of quality and integrity. They also come with lots of fine print and decisions about who and what you support within a well-established consumer structure.

ROOM FOR IMPROVEMENT

Since Gutenberg, the technology of publishing has evolved a great deal. Where publishing hasn't changed is in the legacy institutions and structures created and maintained by the dominant strata of society. Today, the publishing industry consists of *independent publishers* and what we'll call *traditional publishers*.

Independent publishing companies vary in size (some may even be quite large), often have an intentional mission driving their work, and sometimes operate as nonprofit businesses (as in the case of university presses). A Book Apart is a small, independent, for-profit publishing house.

In recent years, traditional publishing companies were dubbed The Big Five—but by the time you read these words, they'll have consolidated into fewer hands yet again. You're likely familiar with their names, like Penguin Random House and Simon & Schuster. They are conglomerates owned by multinational corporations, and they produce the largest percentage of traditionally published books. This means that most mainstream publishing is based in a highly concentrated—and exclusive—power structure. In 2020, the *New York Times* analyzed the racial identities of authors under the biggest publishing conglomerates and found that 95 percent of books published between 1950 and 2018 were written by white people (http://bkaprt.com/ysw40/01-08/, subscription required).

This math sucks. But it's not surprising when the math is reflective of who works in publishing. According to Lee & Low Books' second Diversity Baseline Survey from 2019, the overall publishing industry in North America is 76 percent white, 74 percent cis women, 81 percent heterosexual, and 89 percent non-disabled (http://bkaprt.com/ysw40/01-09/). And A Book Apart, albeit small, is no exception: at the time of writing, our team is 73 percent white. We have a lot more work to do.

It's easy to understand how an aspiring author—especially someone with one or more marginalized identities—would feel not only discouraged and unwelcome before even starting, but unsupported and unrepresented if and once they manage to get inside the industry. Major publishers largely put out books that serve their market interests above anything else, "shaping the discourse" in a way that stakeholders find most palatable and lucrative. And there are unquestionably evil forces working fervently against progress (http://bkaprt.com/ysw40/01-10/).

But the future of publishing isn't hopeless. Change *is* happening. There are dozens of literary orgs and presses who champion (and fund) the work of people of color (http://bkaprt.com/ysw40/01-11/). There are independent presses that actively try to challenge the status quo. And there are more and more tools to put the reins of publishing directly in the hands of writers—and their books directly in the hands of readers.

That's why we're hoping you'll join us in changing things for the better. For everyone. Now.

CLEARING YOUR PATH

As if historical and institutional oppression weren't enough to overcome, there's another obstacle standing in your way: you. Well, more specifically, your doubts and fears. There's no shortage of seemingly good reasons—limited time, work stress, lack of support, imposter syndrome—to *not* do something as big and audacious as writing a book.

You may think those doubts and fears are entirely of your own making, but they actually have roots in societal oppression. One of the key characteristics of white supremacy culture is the idea that there is "one right way," which often shows up as perfectionism, conformity, and an obsession with qualifications (http://bkaprt.com/ysw40/01-12/). We're not going to threaten the status quo if we're convinced we're not qualified or good enough to write a book. We're not gonna set fire to *anything* that way.

But unlike dismantling white supremacy in the publishing industry, dismantling your own insecurities is within your scope. (The former is more of a group project.) Some of our reasons not to write may certainly be valid, but they might also just be lies society is telling us. Let's scrutinize them and see if they hold up:

- **"I'm not an expert."** You don't have to be. Inexperience has advantages: you still remember what it was like to *not* know something, and the sweat and tears that went into learning it. And the experiences you *do* have—even if they're not directly related to your topic—inform your current expertise. Find out what it is that *you* bring to the table that no one else can, and lean into it. Let other people write their books; you write yours.
- **"I don't have all the answers yet."** What if you could think of writing a book not as a way of distributing commandments, but as a method for satiating your own curiosity? Designer and A Book Apart author Dan Brown knows the topic of design discovery like the back of his hand, but he wanted to talk about it in a more intentional and meaningful way with his clients and his team: "Writing *Practical Design Discovery* gave me an opportunity to think deeply about the discovery process," he told us. "I had strong opinions about it, but wanted a well-articulated rationale for those opinions, and a language for talking about discovery." When we think about writing as a channel through which we're working something out, it feels a lot more approachable, exciting, and personal.
- **"I don't know the right people."** Oh, who are the right people, and can you introduce us to them? We kid, but we also know that many folks believe having a connection is the only way to get published. Not true! At A Book Apart, for example, every book proposal goes through the exact same submission process—knowing us personally doesn't skip anyone to the front of the line or result in any special

treatment. And while we can't speak for everyone, we like to think that most publishers consider a book proposal's content beyond just the name at the top. It's always a good idea to build your network, but don't let a lack of "insider status" dissuade you from putting yourself out there.

- **"I don't want to take up space."** You have to take up a little bit of space, okay? In fact, you should take up more space. Your voice is valid; your experience is valid. If you are concerned that you come from a societally dominant group, and that writing a book is taking away space from people in marginalized groups, let's put it this way: writing isn't a zero-sum game. Your stepping out doesn't guarantee someone else stepping in. The best thing you can do is to take up space intentionally and thoughtfully—to use your space to make more space for others. If your voice carries power, don't ignore that; wield it, and wield it for good.
- **"My company isn't comfortable with it."** This can be a tricky needle to thread: to write a book about tech, we often have to draw on the work we do for employers, which can sometimes require permission or negotiating with legal departments. Some employers are enthusiastic and supportive; others are so guarded or litigious that writing a book isn't even an option while you're employed by them. If you think you'd have to hide your book from your employers, that's not just a red flag for your project—that's a red flag for your work environment. You may want to make some changes before formally pursuing your book.
- **"I don't have time."** That's a toughie. Time is a precious resource, and one of the most important ingredients in any big undertaking—but if the thought of eking out even another minute from your schedule makes you need to breathe into a paper bag, now may *not* be the best time to start a book. But that doesn't mean you have to wait until you have a perfect six-month sabbatical lined up either. We'll talk more about time management in Chapter 4.

The only difference between you and the authors who have come before you is just that: they're on the other side of this whole process. And you'll be there one day, too. You don't need to have X years of experience in Y industry, a particular job title, or impressive (by whose standards?) credentials. You certainly don't need to run your own company, have a certain number of LinkedIn connections, or be considered a *thought leader*. Please don't be a thought leader. Just be you.

NOW YOUR TURN

The goal of this book is to encourage you, but as we've just seen, there are a lot of obstacles on the path to authorship. Even if you're an authority on design, development, content, or another discipline, publishing is its own industry with its own history and rules. And life has a sneaky way of blocking the path, too, with all sorts of professional, familial, and social obligations. This whole process is quite the unruly animal—and we haven't even technically started yet.

To overcome the inertia of the publishing industry and ourselves, we need dedication to the work. That commitment can feel daunting to step into, especially if you're still working out what you want to write about. So let's start there: let's look at how to lay a strong foundation for the writing and publishing work ahead.

FROM BRAIN TO BOOK

> *Writing is a conversation with reading; a dialogue with thinking.*
> —NIKKI GIOVANNI

WHEN AUTHOR KAT VELLOS decided to write *We Should Get Together*, her first book about cultivating better adult friendships, she realized that she'd been working on "the book" long before it became apparent it should *be* a book. After years of speaking and giving workshops on the topic, and amassing material through her own writing practice, it turned out that a lot of *book* already existed.

No matter how early you are in your book-planning process, you've been thinking about your topic for a while—maybe even longer than you realize! You've probably been noticing themes in industry conversations, taking note of client concerns or professional dilemmas, or collecting links to articles that set your gears a-turnin'. Maybe you've drafted blog posts or delivered conference talks or tested a few new concepts at company lunch 'n' learns. Maybe you've set up a corkboard and some red yarn. (Listen, we're not judging you. We support your process.)

You're not starting from scratch, even if this is the first time you've thought about writing a book. As A Book Apart author David Dylan Thomas told us:

> *I don't think I've ever stared at a blank page in my life. There's always something before the blank page, before the written form. There are weeks and months of conversation. Before I wrote Design for Cognitive Bias, I had already been thinking about the ideas and coming up with ways to communicate them for three years.*

How do you know when you're ready to make that leap from "a collection of ideas" to "writing a book"? Well, that's up to you, really. But if you've been noodling on an idea for a while, and collecting notes and resources, and drafting your ideas in multiple formats, and reading this book—well, you've already started. Congratulations! We love this journey for you.

DEVELOPING YOUR IDEAS

So what's your book about? Your topic is usually the answer to questions like: What's *interesting* to you? What's keeping you up at night? What are you most drawn to when you're working? Or, heck, what's irritating the hell out of you on the internet? (Many a great book is born of frustration.)

You're not just writing to explain the thing itself—JavaScript, or information architecture, or design systems. There's something you want to say *about* the topic—something you want people to think or do differently in their work. As editor and content strategist Sally Kerrigan put it:

> *When you write about your work, it makes all of us smarter for the effort, including you—because it forces you to go beyond the polite cocktail-party line you use to describe what you do and really think about the impact your work has. Done well, it means you're contributing signal, instead of noise. (http://bkaprt.com/ysw40/02-01/)*

Knowledge and passion are important components, but articulating the signal—the why-you-should-*care* of it all—in a way that will benefit your readers is key. Think about your topic with a few generative questions in mind:

- What's a problem that we haven't yet found a good solution for? Or, what's a solution that has been discarded but should be reconsidered?
- What's a belief, practice, or habit in our industry that isn't serving us (or our users) well? Why should we try to change it? Where do we start?
- What's something about our work that seems to frustrate, confuse, or hold back our colleagues, stakeholders, or clients?
- Where do you see inequity, exclusion, or oppression in our industry? What do we need to change to make things better?
- What recent or upcoming changes in our industry (or in society) will require us to shift our thinking? Where do you see resistance? What can help overcome it?

Answering these questions will help you develop your topic into an argument—that is, a clear point of view, the driving force of your book. Combine that argument with a few other ingredients—like a clear understanding of your audience, their challenges, and your industry context—and you'll have built a strong foundation for your manuscript.

Identify your audience

You are writing *for someone*, so be as specific as possible about who that is. Go beyond "designers" or "people who want to know [thing my book is about]." Consider the roles, backgrounds, and skills your ideal reader might have, and what professional and personal contexts they might be operating in. This has a perfect corollary in web work: How often have you told a client or stakeholder, "The website's audience can't be 'everyone'"? Same goes for you.

When Lisa Maria was in the early stages of planning her first book, *Everyday Information Architecture,* she often thought of a friend who worked as a UX designer. The agency where the friend worked had no designated role for information architecture (IA), so those tasks often fell to her. She told Lisa Maria how frustrating it was to work on sitemaps when IA wasn't part of her training or interests, and how the books from which she sought guidance often seemed too dense or too academic to help her practically.

Lisa Maria also thought about the designers she often collaborated with; they also worked in agency settings, and often had more projects with IA needs than just the ones they had budgeted for her to work on. They too had to take on auditing, sitemap, and taxonomy responsibilities, sometimes without much support.

Between these friends and colleagues, Lisa Maria envisioned her ideal reader as a junior- to mid-level website designer who works on multiple website projects in an agency setting, doesn't have access to IA partners or skill sets, and cares deeply about making better user experiences. *Everyday Information Architecture* started to take shape as a practical guide to help non-IAs get IA tasks done.

Solve problems

You're not just identifying who your audience *is,* but also what they want to *do.* Writing a professional text means you are writing to solve a professional problem your readers are dealing with—why else would they pick up your book?

We often see writers struggle to center their readers when they're first formulating their book ideas (and even well into drafting). We get it—it's tough to approach your ideas from an external perspective, especially when you're jazzed on writing and passionate about your topic. But readers aren't in your head with you, and they don't necessarily share your excitement; if they don't immediately see how your book will benefit them, they won't Add to Cart.

Maybe your audience is junior designers who are struggling to incorporate more research into their process. Maybe it's mid-level JavaScript developers who want to improve performance for low-income users. Maybe it's product managers who are looking for better communication strategies. All of these audiences want to discover something that will help them succeed, and your book needs to give them that. As is so often the case in web work, start with your users' needs.

And to be clear: none of this means your book will *only* be for one type of reader. Your audience will blossom far beyond this starting point as you draft and edit. But by clarifying a specific audience upfront and committing to solving their problems, you set yourself up to keep your writing relevant and actionable, no matter who's reading.

Connect to the conversation

We don't write books in a vacuum—we write them in specific cultural contexts, in specific moments in time, in specific places, and with specific influences. Whatever you write, whether you know it or not, will be in conversation with all the books that came before (and the ones that come after it, too!).

So it's a good idea to know what that discourse looks like. What other books have been published on your topic? What articles have been written? What are folks saying about this topic on social media? What trends or controversies in your discipline are you affirming or challenging? What points of connection does your topic have to other industries?

Being able to answer these questions will bolster your ideas in many ways:

- You'll find potential new sources of expertise for your research.
- You'll boost your authority by being able to cite more (and more varied) practitioners.
- You'll spot gaps in industry knowledge that your book could help to fill.
- You'll know how your book is different from what's already out there, or, if not, how to make it different.

You'll also be better informed about the commercial landscape when it comes time to pitch (and eventually market) your book. You might be surprised at how often A Book Apart receives pitches claiming that no other books on their topic exist—even though our own catalog contains exactly that. Don't be that person. Read (or at least learn about) other books related to your topic, especially the ones from any publishers you might want to work with.

We're hard-pressed to think of a topic that doesn't already have books written about it—but that's not a problem! Your goal isn't to come up with the world's most original topic; your goal is to add your voice to the conversation. You can build on ideas found in earlier books, the way Eva PenzeyMoog's *Design for Safety* referenced Eric Meyer and Sara Wachter-Boettcher's *Design for Real Life*. Or you might differentiate your book from a similar one by changing audience or scale; for example, Beth Dunn's *Cultivating Content Design* is aimed at individual contributors trying to establish content design practices in their organizations, while Rachel McConnell's *Leading Content Design* speaks to content leads about operationalizing many of those same practices.

Professional texts are in constant dialogue with one another. You don't need a fully-fledged competitive marketing plan—just be familiar with the current industry landscape.

BUILDING YOUR NARRATIVE

Once you've done some thinking about your topic, your readers, and your context, it's time to mold that thinking into something that resembles a book—that is, how it might work as a written narrative experience.

All books have a *narrative*. That doesn't mean you're telling an explicit *story* (though you can!). It means there's a beginning, a middle, and an end, with a conceptual path for readers to follow. The narrative is a way of imposing order on what would otherwise be a jumble of thoughts and abstract concepts—a way of layering your ideas so that they gradually add up to a larger meaning.

If your book, like this one, describes a process, then the topics will likely be linear and chronological. But even if your book is more modular—say, the chapters can be read in any order, or readers are meant to jump in cold to the sections most relevant to their own work—you should still have some rationale for the order in which your ideas are presented.

This is a good point in your journey to start mixing in some structure. What might the beginning, middle, and end look like for your book? What do your readers (your users!) want to learn, and which concepts do they need to learn first to understand the others? Your narrative—the way you present, order, and build your concepts—determines how your readers will move through the material.

Make a plan

Outlines are probably the best-known way of planning out any piece of writing: most of us were forced to use them in school, and, for many writers, they become an anxiety-reducing device in professional contexts. They're orderly and methodical—predictable comfort in a chaotic world. They take your intentions for your book and promise to hold you accountable to them.

Outlines are excellent tools for planning out three crucial aspects of your writing:

- **Narrative progression:** An outline maps the order of your subjects, starting with introductory ideas at the top, progressing through a logical flow, and ending with your concluding thoughts. You can plot out how your ideas build on one another and determine where you might need to rearrange your ideas or change the pace of your discussion.
- **Conceptual hierarchy:** Since each line represents a major topic, theme, or idea, and each indent represents increasingly granular detail, you can use an outline to track how your ideas connect to one another—which ones are bigger and broader (the chapter level) and which ones do the supporting work (sections and subsections).

- **Your own efforts:** If you know what you want to write about, but aren't sure how to present it, a good outline can act as a series of prompts to begin drafting, or can help you clarify what to work on when. Essentially, an outline chunks your drafting into manageable pieces (which we'll talk about more in Chapter 4).

An outline is a blueprint for your narrative, but think sandcastle, not condo: the planning and the writing will push back on each other throughout your process. Designer Shara Rosenbalm described her writing process to us this way:

> It's iterative. It's like building a product. We have to be nimble. We have to be flexible. We have to be prepared to pivot. Our plan might be pretty, and we might have emotional attachment to it. But we're setting ourselves up for failure if we're not ready to change.

Change is constant! Keep your outline as flexible (or as rigid) as is useful for you. You may find that your outline helps kick things off, and then, like an action hero walking away from an explosion, you never look back at it again as you draft. Or you may find that updating the outline as you write—using it to stay on topical track—works well for you.

But not everyone likes outlines. Some of you downright despise them. How dare we restrict your ideas to tiny, hierarchical boxes that give them no room to discover their true selves? When they turn eighteen, they are *so* outta here.

If outlines don't work for your brain, that's okay! Author Krystal Higgins told A Book Apart:

> For me, creativity and plans are mutually exclusive; I like to follow the threads of new ideas as I get hands-on into a project. That has its upsides (lots of wacky ideas, helps me connect the dots at a systems level) and downsides (hello, distractions!). In the writing world, they call writers who outline "plotters" and those who fly by the seats of their pants "pantsers." I'm certainly a pantser, [though] I admire the plotters in the world. (http://bkaprt.com/ysw40/02-02/)

Higgins put together an outline for *Better Onboarding* for her book proposal; it's required for our submissions process, but not for her writing process. Similarly, Jennifer Peepas of captainawkward.com confessed in a post to Patreon subscribers:

> *I have never once made an outline of a thing and then made that intended thing from the outline, not even when I was first taught to do outlines in 5th grade. Every time I have ever had an outline due before an assignment, I made a draft of the assignment, built the outline from it, turned that in, got notes, and then turned in a revised assignment, which was doubtless improved by the process. It was the same for my book proposal—I built a shadow manuscript in Scrivener out of existing posts and then moved them around until they seemed like chapters, THEN I wrote the "proposed chapter outline."* (http://bkaprt.com/ysw40/02-03/)

If you are among the outline-averse, know that there are all sorts of creative exercises out there for meaning-making and structure-imposing. We are limited in what we can personally recommend, as we are both outline enthusiasts, but we support you and your ability to think beyond the outline. We don't understand you, but we support you!

Arrange your ideas

While an outline (or your planning tool of choice) can help you keep track of what goes where, it can't tell you what *should* go where. We can't, either. Cool book we wrote here!

Realistically, the flow of your book will depend on the specifics of your topic, your overall scope, and your approach. That said, you're probably aware that you should start broad, then add detail, then wrap up. Many books about technical topics follow similar narrative arcs:

- **The beginning** (the first chapter or two, with or without a separate introduction) presents the topic's key concepts and definitions. Sometimes it contextualizes the topic within the industry, disciplinary practices, or history. It's also important to explain up front why the topic matters (though the *why* will likely be woven throughout the narrative as well).

- **Middle chapters** usually get into the particulars of the work itself: the techniques, tools, frameworks, processes, and new ways of thinking that you're recommending to readers. This is the meat of the book—what we might call the *what,* with a good dose of the *how.*
- **Later chapters** continue the *how* in more granular detail, often looking to set the reader up for success: how to integrate new tactics into the reader's workflow, how to convince stakeholders to support new design or development practices, or how to work with clients or team members in a new way. The final chapter or conclusion may discuss the future of the topic, and revisit the *why* in a new light.

This loose, flexible narrative structure can work well for a lot of topics. It shows up often in A Book Apart books (which tend to be pedagogical or process-based), but that doesn't mean *every* book should follow that path, or that it's appropriate for every topic. Play around with presentation order and flow to see what suits your ideas best.

Shape your story

Gosh, humans sure love a story. Order, presentation, and structure are all fine and dandy, but nothing draws people in the way a good story can—and that holds true for articles, conference talks, and, yes, technical books. Even if your topic is technical or academic, telling engaging, relatable stories can attract readers and keep them around long enough to learn something. (Try a sword fight. Bonus points if the sword fight is waged by necromancers in outer space.)

A little bit of excitement can go a long way, and that's where thinking in terms of storytelling—conflict, solutions, rising and falling action—can give your book more oomph than a basic chapter hierarchy can. In *Show and Tell,* speaker Dan Roam argues that there are only four available storylines for any given presentation:

- *The Report: The report brings data to life. With a report, we change our audience's information.*
- *The Explanation: The explanation shows us how. With an explanation, we change our audience's knowledge or ability.*
- *The Pitch: The pitch gets us over the hurdle. With a pitch, we change our audience's actions.*
- *The Drama: The drama breaks our heart, then mends it. With a drama, we change our audience's beliefs.*

And while Roam's guidance is meant for crafting talks, it's equally valuable for shaping your book—particularly if you're having trouble pinning down a cohesive narrative or identifying a single way forward. Roam suggests asking yourself a very straightforward question:

> *To pick the right storyline, all we need to do is answer the following question: "After we've finished presenting, how do we want our audience to be different from when we started?"* (http://bkaprt.com/ysw40/02-04/)

Your answer should point you toward a viable storyline for your narrative. Many books written about working with technology are likely to resemble The Explanation or The Pitch; books like Krystal Higgins's *Better Onboarding* or Yesenia Perez-Cruz's *Expressive Design Systems* are meant to shift their readers' design abilities and actions. Books like Eva PenzeyMoog's *Design for Safety* or Senongo Akpem's *Cross-Cultural Design* are similar, but with a touch of The Drama, because they ask their readers to change their beliefs about their work.

What we like about this approach is that it focuses on what the audience needs. Many potential authors feel passionate about their big idea, but if they can't make it matter to their readers, that passion will have nowhere to go. Ultimately, this is about remembering whom the book is for and what they'll need to do after they've read it—not just what you want to say.

PRACTICE MAKES PERFECT

Haven't we done enough prep work? you might be asking. *Can't we just dive into the drafting already? Can't we just get started?* To which we reply: *Listen, stop, just be cool for, like, a minute.* We need to talk about the writing that happens before the writing.

The scandalous, shocking truth is that most of us aren't professional writers. We are designers, developers, project managers, and researchers. Even if we are copywriters or content designers—literally making a living from wordcraft—we write within very specific, externalized contexts. Most web professionals write regularly to communicate ideas to users, clients, colleagues, potential employers, stakeholders, etc.—but that's not the same as writing a book's worth of personal prose.

Writing a book is also an entirely different kind of writing from what most of us are used to—not just in length (obviously, a book is not a button label), but in tone, audience, approach, and goal. Which means that no matter how much writing you've done on the job, *you've never done this.*

Of course, you can and you *will*—but you may need more rehearsal than you think. Not only do you have to warm up the part of your brain that makes words go (that's a technical term), but you also need to prepare for what happens when those words show up outside of yourself. Let's look at a few habits that can benefit your book before you even start to draft it.

You are what you read

It's the oldest and most boring advice in the book (literally), but it's also the truest: reading improves writing.

First, reading exposes you to different ideas, perspectives, and voices, which enrich and challenge your own thinking. Cross-pollinating your thoughts with others' can lead to all sorts of new and improved concepts. The key is to draw on a wide range of perspectives. The tech industry attracts people from every background imaginable, so take advantage of that richness by consuming work created by people whose lives don't look like yours. (And, in fairness, reading doesn't have a monopoly on that specific benefit—podcasts, audiobooks, video games, poetry, and visual art will similarly engage your brain.)

Second, you strengthen your own craft, style, and voice when you study the way other writers write. That might mean conscious study—really paying attention to how a writer wields words, explains concepts, establishes tone, or controls the narrative. But it can also happen through well-applied immersion, which is why writers always make the same recommendation: *just keep reading.*

We recommend reading anything and everything—from tweets to fanfic to personal essays to tech blogs—but you'll benefit most from exposure to the kind of writing you want to emulate. Read work by authors whose style you admire; authors who write in ways you find engaging, approachable, understandable, and even inspiring; authors who can break down complex ideas in clear, useful ways (especially if you're writing about a technical topic). Learn how they teach readers through writing so you can do the same.

Bottom line: your input influences your output. If you want to write a thoughtful, inclusive, sharply written text, surround yourself with thoughtful, inclusive, sharply written texts.

Start a writing practice

Kat Vellos had an established writing practice when she began developing *We Should Get Together,* but it wasn't made up of a singular activity. She journaled, she wrote to document what she thought and experienced, and she sought out writing circles to get feedback and accountability. She used a variety of approaches and tools so she could stay connected to her practice in a way that felt both practical and creative.

You can do the same. Building a consistent writing habit will both improve your writing skills and get you accustomed to the regular practice that drafting requires. You might try:

- **Writing sprints:** In *Cultivating Content Design,* Beth Dunn suggests thirty-day writing sprints, on your own or with others: "The goal is to get comfortable with the practice of dumping words out of your brain. [You] can worry about the editing and shaping of it later. The stripped-down version of this writing sprint practice is really: 1. write like crap, 2. every day, 3. about not much at all." The writing itself doesn't matter—what matters is the *act* of writing, daily, for a month.

- **Morning pages:** Morning pages are another daily writing ritual, but with the goal of hitting a specific number of words, pages, or minutes each morning. The practice, created by Julia Cameron in *The Artist's Way* (http://bkaprt.com/ysw40/02-05/), may feel like sprints day to day, but is more like a marathon, meant to go the distance. Where writing sprints might be done in groups for accountability, morning pages are more personal, often dipping into stream of consciousness or self-reflection in an effort to clear the mind for more intentional writing.

- **Journal prompts:** Whether you are writing daily or not, another great way to practice writing is to respond to journal prompts. While sprints and morning pages encourage uncensored brain dumps, journal prompts provoke more structured, narrative writing. Prompts can be anything from a single word, to multiple questions, to full-on instructions— anything that sparks a response. (See the Resources section for a few starting points, though your closest search engine will have plenty more.)

None of these tactics is meant to produce polished writing or bits of your book. Their purpose is to establish a regular, reproduceable, and *comfortable* habit that paves the way for the later labor of drafting.

Put it out there

Writing for yourself is an excellent practice, but you also need to understand how to write *out loud*. If you haven't shared your writing publicly before, now's the time. Spreading your ideas around will net you all kinds of generative feedback. You'll learn how your communication style comes across to strangers, what aspects of your thinking you need to develop, and where you might need to do more research.

There are plenty of options for putting your work out there, but let's take them one level at a time:

- **Bite-sized:** The quickest way to share your ideas is through social platforms. Social media's brevity probably won't improve your writing skills, but you'll find out (whether you want to or not, frankly) exactly how other people react to your ideas. Proceed with caution, though, as many online communities are rife with hostility and lacking in oversight; stick to platforms where you're already active and understand the culture.
- **Chapter-sized:** Blog posts, articles, and newsletters are all excellent formats for exploring both your ideas and your writing skills—enough space to expand on your thoughts, but not so much that you're writing a whole book yet. The advantage of blog posts and newsletters is that they are completely within your control, from start to finish. Articles published through media outlets, on the other hand, may involve a pitching process—but such outlets will also reach more readers than you can alone.
- **Stage-sized:** At A Book Apart, it's common for us to see book proposals from folks who have never written a book before but *have* given a conference talk on their topic. Although the two formats couldn't be more different, what they have in common is a willingness to develop ideas for an audience. Public speaking—through conference talks, internal presentations at your company, and local meetups—is an excellent way to push your thinking, gather feedback, and refine your material based on your audience's needs.

Writing about your topic in smaller bites will help you identify your areas of interest and working knowledge. Over the course of months or even years, you'll hone those ideas, make theoretical connections, and build up a library of resources to draw on when it comes time to develop a book outline or proposal. These formats will also come in handy when you're marketing your book (see Chapter 7), so building up your experience and networks now will continue to reap rewards.

As you share your ideas publicly, reflect on your experiences with each medium. What worked well about each one, and what didn't? Did readers react the way you expected? Is there a technical concept you're still trying to work out? How did your thinking change with each iteration? Your insights here can teach you to adapt your material in response to changing contexts, audience needs, and formats—which you'll definitely need to do for a book.

Line up supporters

Feedback on your ideas is invaluable, but it's not the only reason to share your work with others. You also want folks in your corner—now, as you're shaping your initial ideas; and later, as you write, revise, and market the results. Writer and scholar Jenn M. Jackson sees her supporters as a crucial element in successful writing projects:

> *Share your writing with people you trust who will thoughtfully and carefully challenge you to push yourself. These are not detractors and naysayers (avoid those). These are supporters who believe in the work, the vision, and the goals. (http:// bkaprt.com/ysw40/02-06/)*

Different kinds of relationships can provide you with different kinds of support. Do you have other authors in your life? Ask them what the drafting and publishing process was like for them. Do you have colleagues with strong written communication skills? Ask them for constructive criticism on yours. Do you have mentors or friends who want to shower you with enthusiasm and encouragement? Turn to them for cheerleading.

If you want more structured or formal development of your writing, join a writing group (http://bkaprt.com/ysw40/02-07/). Writing groups may be casual get-togethers focused on account-ability, lunch check-ins with coworkers, professional writing critiques, and everything in between. They span (and may mix) genres, experience levels, skill levels, and meeting styles. The key is to find a group whose goals and values match yours. If you're writing a book about web work, you may want to find others writing about technology—but you don't have to. Good communication is good communication on most any topic, so consider what you want to get out of the group and choose (or create!) accordingly.

AUTOBOTS, ROLL OUT!

Share your ideas, take in feedback, and iterate, iterate, iterate: that's how you get from a wild little seed of an idea to something that might feel like a book in the making. All this preparation is leading to your next course of action: determining how your book might show up in the world, whether that means putting together a book proposal to send out to publishers, or laying the groundwork for self-publishing before you start drafting. That's where we're heading next.

3 CHOOSE YOUR OWN ADVENTURE

> " If there's a book that you want to read, but it hasn't been written yet, then you must write it.
> —TONI MORRISON

WHEN CONTENT STRATEGIST Corey Vilhauer and developer Deane Barker wrote their book *The Web Project Guide*, it wasn't a book at all—it was a website. They wrote and published each chapter online, in real time, as a completely free resource.

It was only after the chapters were complete that they decided to consider a printed version—and then they couldn't find a publisher. "We had written a book that we were really proud of, and nobody wanted it," Vilhauer told us. Because the book was written for nontechnical audiences as an overview of everything that goes into making a website, it "was too technical for general publishers, and not technical enough for tech publishers. That was hard." Undaunted, Vilhauer and Barker hired a small company to walk them through the production process—getting an ISBN, making the book available through online retailers—and did all their own design and promotion.

Now their work exists as both a tangible, sellable paperback and an editable, adaptable website (http://bkaprt.com/ysw40/03-

01/). The print book exists as "more of a snapshot of the specific moment in time when it went to print, while the online version can grow and expand."

Vilhauer's experience shows that there's no right or wrong way to publish a book these days. Print or digital, traditional or DIY—if you want to write a book, there are many paths to get there. It's all about your choices.

YOU CAN GET WITH THIS, OR YOU CAN GET WITH THAT

At a high level, there are two primary paths to publishing your book: self-publishing, or working with an established publisher. There are benefits and drawbacks to both options.

Self-publishing gives you total control over the process; there are no gatekeepers in the way, and no one will reject your ideas. On the other hand, you'll have to find your own partners in editing or marketing (if that's important to your goals), and you'll be responsible for printing and distributing the book (or managing the digital files). And, as you might imagine, working with other professionals and service providers will cost time and money.

Working with a publisher means you'll have the support of a publishing house for bringing your book to life—from working with established editors to getting marketing guidance. It means you likely won't incur any personal expenses to write your book. It also means you'll have to go through the process of pitching your book and having someone agree to publish it— and you'll have to work within their structures and timelines.

Self-publishing

If your book-publishing dreams feature *you* valiantly leading the way forward at every step, self-publishing is a great option. In *The Developer's Guide to Book Publishing*, Stephanie Morillo succinctly explains the benefits—and responsibilities—that come with self-publishing:

Self-publishing is a hands-on process, giving authors more control of the end-to-end production process, from how much to charge to the art direction. Everything you can count on a publisher to do—editing a manuscript, designing a book cover, managing distribution, and marketing your book—now falls on you. (http://bkaprt.com/ysw40/03-02/)

Do not psych yourself out of this route! Self-publishing is absolutely, totally doable. You can still get the marketing, development, and editorial help that you'd normally get from a publisher; you just have to build that world yourself. We'll explain those nuts and bolts in later chapters.

For now, let's look at the most important considerations when it comes to deciding to self-publish. Think about how much time, energy, and financial resources you can (or want to) afford to support the following:

- **Editing:** No matter how strong of a writer you are, your manuscript *will* need editing. What that looks like may vary, from self-editing with some free resources (like what you'll find in Chapter 5), to asking subject-matter experts for reviews, to hiring freelance editors. Editing will make your book intrinsically better. You'll want to research costs for hiring and working with a professional editor or two.
- **Production and distribution:** How will your book be created and sent to readers? Whether you publish in print or digital formats, you'll need a basic design for your book—and you'll need to budget for a designer if you're not comfortable doing it yourself. When it comes to paper books, you'll want to consider print-on-demand or upfront printing and distribution costs; luckily there are now lots of services that do some or all of this. If you're going to go through the work of editing, designing, and producing your book—and if the time, effort, and budget fit—it'll be worth making it available in digital formats as well.

In all cases, working with other professionals will cost money, and doing it on your own will cost time; it's a matter of weighing what works for you. It's like when you rent out a room at a restaurant for a big dinner party and they have all the tables, chairs, linens, and food already there—versus when you tell all the partygoers to meet up at the park and bring something because it's potluck style, and please let's just hope Chad remembers the salsa this time. *Get it together, Chad.* We've got a book to make.

Working with a publisher

If self-publishing doesn't feel like the right fit, perhaps working with a publisher is more your style. Working with a publisher is a great path to pursue, and we're going to spend the rest of this chapter exploring the process of approaching and pitching to publishers.

Start by researching which publishers you might want to work with. There are dozens (and sometimes hundreds) of publishers producing books like the one you're writing, depending on the topic, audience, and approach. Start by exploring who publishes your favorite books. Which publishers attract the types of readers you'd like to reach? What do you like about their mission, values, or presence in the tech industry or writing community?

WHAT PUBLISHERS WANT

If you've decided you want to work with an established publisher, your next step is to prepare a book proposal—the only way to get your idea in front of the people who can make it happen.

Broadly speaking, publishers want to see that you've gone beyond "I've got a book idea!" to really thinking through what the book can and will be. At A Book Apart, we want to know about:

- **You.** We want to know some basic info about who you are. Yes, we want to read your professional bio if you have one; that's always helpful. We also want to know what you feel your greatest strengths are to write the book you're proposing—in your words, what's important here? And heck, we also want to know why you want to write for and publish with us. What is it about our publishing house that drew you and your book idea in?

- **Your book.** This is where we get to see the *shape* of your book—through things like the elevator pitch, chapter outline, and any sample writing—and how you're setting out to approach crafting it. We also ask questions about the book topic's importance, the book's possible positioning in the market, your method of gathering research, and any known competition. All of this helps us understand your broader thinking about how you envision the *life* of the book, how it will be composed, and how it might exist in the world.
- **The marketing opportunity.** Here's where we dig into how you might most successfully sell your book—and how *we* can help with that. We want to know how you communicate with your existing audience, how to reach more readers, and how we can leverage your unique network to help the book thrive.

A meaningful book proposal will ultimately answer this question: "How will sharing your experiences make your reader's life better or different?" It should showcase your voice and your goals clearly and confidently. Proposals are typically constructed from a few crucial elements:

- **Working title.** A tentative book title. It doesn't have to be perfect, but hopefully it's interesting, catchy, and indicative of what's to come.
- **Thesis.** The concise statement or theory you're putting forth as a premise to be proved or maintained. Think back to the argument you developed in Chapter 2!
- **Elevator pitch.** A concise summary of what your book is about and what it will do for readers. The elevator pitch works to sell your thesis.
- **Table of contents.** An outline of your chapters or a table of contents tells publishers what content you'll cover and how you'll structure the book.

Every publisher is different, and each one will likely want to see a varying combination of the proposal elements we've described. Some may require sample chapters or even a full rough draft. Others (like ABA) may want to see a detailed outline for each chapter. Some publishers may even require social media networks of a certain size, in-depth audience research, and marketing plans. That's why it's important to do a bit of publisher research instead of writing a one-size-fits-all proposal.

If you have a working title, a thesis, an elevator pitch, and a table of contents or an outline, you'll be able to adapt your proposal to include the specific requirements of whichever publisher you pitch to. Let's take a closer look at those key proposal elements.

Working title

You probably won't know the (final) title of your book until you've finished writing it—that's why it's called a *working* title. Most of the books we publish at A Book Apart wind up with a title that's pretty different from where it started. (Heck, this book's working title was *Book Book* until we were about halfway through editing!) That's why it's fun to dream up names for what you're going to call this labor of love, for now. You might even come back to this bit after you have the rest of your pitch together.

There's an urge to get overly creative here, but one thing we've learned along the way is that you really can't go wrong with plain language. For example, if your book is about doing just enough research to do better design, why not call it *Just Enough Research*? If it's about using JavaScript responsibly, why not *Responsible JavaScript*? You get the idea.

Just don't agonize too much! The working title can help frame your (and your potential publisher's) thinking, but it's meant to flex. The journey is much more enjoyable if you allow a little room for the final title to emerge as you develop the book. (And if you're working with a publisher, remember that they typically have the final say on the title.)

Thesis

A thesis is traditionally defined as the central argument or "big idea" around which you're building your writing. It's not only a key part of your book pitch, but, more important, it's a guiding light to keep you aligned internally as you develop your idea and begin writing. Having a clearly articulated thesis is often the difference between a strong first draft and one that's muddy and meandering.

Your thesis should be concise—a single-sentence argument. Think of it as a summary of your main point or claim. Short as it is, it can feel, well, big. A good place to start is by breaking down your thesis into two key elements: your topic and your perspective on it.

For example, Jeremy Wagner's thesis for *Responsible JavaScript* could be written as:

> *JavaScript should be used with care to create user experiences that are fast, durable, and delightful.*

His topic was JavaScript, but his perspective was that it was a resource to be used carefully—more carefully than he was seeing in practice. Everything in his book tied back to the argument that developer practices around JavaScript need to change.

Similarly, a line from the introduction to *SEO for Everyone* makes an excellent thesis:

> *Addressing search in digital projects deserves a thoughtful approach that focuses on meeting user needs and delivering a better experience—what we call human-centered SEO.*

Rebekah Baggs and Chris Corak were writing about SEO but had a very specific argument to make about the role of SEO in design projects. They even went so far as to coin a term for their approach—human-centered SEO—but you don't need neologisms so long as you're articulating a clear perspective.

Another good example comes from Beth Dunn's proposal for *Cultivating Content Design*:

*Content practitioners can make more headway in their organi-
zations by inviting more people into their practice, empowering
others to use content to achieve business goals, and adopting a
"we're all in this together" mindset.*

Her topic was content practices in organizations, but her
thesis identified why that topic matters to readers and what she
hopes they'll do about it. And when you start thinking about
what your reader is going to learn from your argument, well,
you're halfway to writing your elevator pitch.

Elevator pitch

An *elevator pitch* is a brief paragraph that summarizes the entire
book. It's like an expansion of your thesis: while the thesis is a
single-sentence argument at the heart of your book, the elevator
pitch is in the business of selling. It should have a compelling
hook and include who your audience is, what their challenge
is, and, *crucially*, how your book will help them solve it.

There's a reason the elevator pitch concept is so valuable:
if you can't express your idea in a few sentences, you risk
losing the attention of publishers (and readers) who are deciding between your book and dozens of others. We know that
sounds a little corporate, but humans have short attention
spans; they're busy worrying about rent and dinner and vacci-
nation schedules. Make the decision to read your book an easy
and immediate one.

Take a look at the elevator pitch for *SEO for Everyone*:

*User-centered SEO isn't just some magic you sprinkle on fin-
ished web copy right before hitting publish. SEO components—
like search intent, internal linking structures, content hierarchy,
structured data, and meta descriptions—are built into content
design decisions. Learn how to add a search-strategy lens to
the content research and design work you already do, without
compromising user experience, and understand how, when, and
where SEO essentials play into your workflow.*

Compare that to the thesis we saw earlier. The elevator pitch is longer—three sentences as opposed to one—and it reads a little like a back-of-the-book summary. It's also written to the reader, identifying who they might be (content and design practitioners), the problem at hand (when SEO conflicts with UX work), how the reader can solve it (by learning to incorporate SEO considerations into the process they already have), and why that will benefit them (no more compromising the UX!).

Similarly, look at the elevator pitch for *Cultivating Content Design*:

> *Bird by Bird for the content design world. How to build a thriving content design practice from solo practitioner to a fully integrated, well-funded team. How to change your own mindset from one of scarce resources and no leverage into a vision of content that feeds the growth and health of each team, each department, each person at your organization.*

It's very different from *SEO for Everyone*—it's not even complete sentences! But it has the same elements: who (content design solo practitioners), what (building a well-resourced team), how (changing mindset), and why (to create a thriving practice).

There are many ways to write an elevator pitch, but one thing you might try is literally explaining your book idea out loud to someone else (it doesn't have to be in an elevator). You're trying to keep it conversational, yet promotional, in three sentences or less. If you find you're meandering, or it's hard to get to the point, or the person you're sharing it with doesn't seem intrigued, that may be a signal to revisit your thesis. Circle back to your argument and think again about why you care about your topic, and—crucially—what problem you're trying to help readers solve.

Table of contents

A high-level table of contents (TOC) illustrates your book's main concepts and provides an at-a-glance sense of structure and flow. It demonstrates the full scope of your material much more clearly than the elevator pitch alone.

At A Book Apart, we like to see as much detail as possible in the proposed TOC. More than just a list of topics, we're looking for the arguments to be made in each chapter, the kinds of details that will support those arguments, and hints of the connective tissue that will bring them all together. Remember your thesis statement—everything in the TOC should support it!

In the proposal for *Cross-Cultural Design*, Senongo Akpem prepared an excellent TOC that bulleted his key topics under each chapter title, as you can see from the outline of his second chapter:

Chapter 2: Cultural Variables in Design
- *Geert Hofstede and the Development of Cultural Variables*
  - *Variable 1: High-Context versus Low-Context Cultures*
  - *Variable 2: Fast-Messaging versus Slow-Messaging Cultures*
  - *Variable 3: Ambiguity versus Directness*
  - *Variable 4: Collectivism versus Individualism*
  - *Variable 5: High-Power-Distance versus Low-Power-Distance Cultures*
- *Ways to Use These Variables as Part of Creation*
- *Dos and Don'ts of Cultural Variables*

And while this told us a lot about the content of that chapter, we weren't entirely sure what the phrase "cultural variables" was meant to convey to readers. So before accepting his pitch, we asked him to provide us with a few more details for each chapter. Here's what he added to the second chapter:

This chapter examines the different cultural variables that are important for understanding design. It explains them at a high level, then goes into depth about how they can be used visually. It also defines the caveats that come with any discussion of

culture and nationhood, by clarifying how societies organize
themselves and how individuals organize themselves.
  Key Takeaways
   • *Understand the ways that cultural variables are*
     researched and determined
   • *Understand all the key variables by name*
   • *Be able to identify cultural traits that affect design,*
     content strategy, and visual culture

He prepared an elevator pitch and three key lessons for readers for each chapter, which created a very thorough outline. Not every publisher requires that level of detail (and some require more), but it certainly doesn't hurt to explain exactly what you're hoping to achieve, to whatever degree of fidelity you need.

TOCs can be proof that you've done the work of thinking *through* the thesis, that you know how your big idea will be presented, argued, and supported. The level of detail you choose to share will depend on your style and the publisher, but we recommend using your TOC as a tool (like everything else in your pitch) for helping publishers make an informed decision.

SUBMITTING YOUR PROPOSAL

You've just spent all this time putting together a thoughtful proposal, you care deeply about the subject matter, and you're ready to share it with the world. *Heckin' yes!*

This is maybe the step that feels scariest. It means you will open yourself up to opportunity—and rejection. But! There *are* some steps you can take to be as thoughtful and intentional as possible about sharing your proposal, which can increase your chances of getting a publisher's attention and buy-in.

First, get a second set of peepers on your proposal. If you have professional or peer feedback available to you while you craft your proposal, take advantage of it! It's always okay to ask for help, and more often than not, getting input on a creative endeavor makes the finished product even better (and makes for a far less lonely experience). At the very least, send your proposal to a trusted friend to proofread (as in: look for grammatical mistakes and typos) and to tell you whether the proposal is clear and easy to read.

Take any feedback to heart. No one knows your book idea better than you do, but it helps to hear some fresh perspectives that haven't been bouncing around inside your skull with you this whole time. Consider their suggestions and revise your proposal as needed.

Head over to your chosen publishers' sites and scour their submission requirements. Most publishers have a proposal form, and sometimes they'll explain what their pitch process is. Spend some time getting to know their specific requirements, and *always* follow directions. (*Psst*: A Book Apart's submission form is available right on our website (http://bkaprt.com/ysw40/03-03/).

Finally, a quick request: please don't spam arbitrary publishers with your proposal! Of course *you* would never do this—but publishers constantly receive proposals for all sorts of ill-fitting book ideas that don't match their niche, mission, or audience. This sort of scattershot strategy makes publishers think, *Hm, this writer isn't paying attention, or they don't care whose inbox their proposal actually landed in.*

How proposals are vetted

Once you've sent your proposal in, you can just sit back and chill. Waiting to hear back from publishers is a super-relaxing period of time that you definitely won't spend glued to your screen, refreshing your inbox every seventeen seconds. Nope. Nobody's doing that.

The waiting game is rough, but it does offer an opportunity to reflect on the fact that you have officially pitched a book proposal! Since there's nothing you can do to speed up publishers' responses (we promise), instead, let's talk about what's potentially going on at the other end of that submission form.

Well, every publisher is different, of course. Proposals may go directly to a specific editor's inbox, or to a general inbox that different editors access. There may be a schedule for reading new proposals (e.g., once a week, once a month) or they may be read on a rolling basis. There may be one person responsible for accepting or declining submissions, or there may be a board that votes, or there may be a handful of editors who discuss and decide.

The vetting process is imbued with a lot of subjectivity, which makes it easy prey for sexism, racism, and elitism. Even though there are organized, structured processes in place, they are created by people who work in and benefit from a system that is historically oppressive and gatekeeper-y. People, though well-intentioned, are fallible, especially when it comes to making judgments about something like "fit" while attempting to acknowledge and navigate their own biases. (That includes us.)

We want this to change; you probably do too. We're working every day to change the way we operate within ourselves and our publishing practices at ABA. While we can't speak for other publishers, it helps to recognize the landscape—and we've learned that making change requires slowing down, unlearning, and practicing all the time.

Publishers have wide-ranging criteria for deciding whether to take on a book project—but here are some common (though by no means exhaustive or universal) factors that many publishers will be thinking about when reading your proposal:

- **Publisher fit.** Overall fit of the book within the publisher's catalog, considering things like genre, audience, content, style, values, approach, and voice and tone.
- **Market fit.** How the book will or can be positioned and sold to the publisher's existing market, as well as new, overlapping, or adjacent markets.
- **Subject-matter relevance.** Whether the book's subject matter is relevant to what the publisher wants to include in their catalog and is marketable to their audience.
- **Topic timeliness, stability, and endurance.** Whether the topic is timely (is it a current, evolving issue or theme?), stable (is the topic evergreen?), and enduring (does the topic have potential to have a long market life?).

- **Writer ability and potential.** How experienced the author is as a writer, researcher, and collaborator. You might want (or be asked) to provide writing samples to help paint a better picture of the book and give a sense of your writing style and technique.

These criteria may differ from publisher to publisher, and—even more important to know—they may be *weighted* differently from publisher to publisher, or even within a publishing house from pitch to pitch.

Which is all to say: it is possible to write a good book proposal and be rejected. It is also possible to write a not-as-good book proposal and be accepted. It's not that there's no rhyme or reason to the process! It's just that different factors may matter in different ways and at different times. Know that whatever response you get back from a publisher, it's not a personal referendum on *you*.

SEARCHING FOR SIGNAL

If your proposal submission is seemingly met with the sound of crickets, it's not necessarily the end of the road, and it's okay to follow up. If you get a canned response (which is totally normal) and a few weeks go by, reach out again. Publishers are often overwhelmed with pitches (and, you know, *publishing*) and sometimes it takes longer than anticipated before they can get a reply to you. Just because you don't hear back right away doesn't mean they're not interested.

Dealing with "no"

There is nothing so confirming of our human existence as a dose of rejection. It is part of life. A not-so-great-feeling part of life, but an expected one. There are tons of ways to try to synthesize and cope with rejection, but we'll be real here: rejection sucks.

It is, however, absolutely live-through-able—and sometimes it helps us refine, reassess, or redirect our ideas. One of our favorite authors, Keah Brown, says it best:

I think that you just have to look at rejections as stepping stones to either something greater, something different, or just a moment in time when you were not ready and they were not ready for you. (http://bkaprt.com/ysw40/03-04/)

Editors reject pitches for any number of reasons, many of which aren't about you or are beyond your control—which means there are likely plenty of good things going on in your pitch. Maybe the editors didn't agree with your premise but liked how you structured your narrative—which tells you about your strengths. Maybe they thought your pitch was compelling but didn't match their mission—which means you might find success with a publisher who's more aligned with your vision. Lean into what seems to be working, and don't be afraid to let go of what isn't getting positive reactions.

One tangible way to alchemize a pass on a proposal is to ask for feedback. Some publishers will provide feedback as part of their rejection communication, to help you understand why your proposal wasn't a fit. Many publishers do *not* offer feedback, usually because their proposal intake is voluminous and they don't have the resources to give feedback on every pitch. It's completely reasonable and valid for you to ask for feedback; the worst that can happen is that they say no, which, hey, you've already been through that!

If you receive feedback, take it gracefully; say thank you and move on. Feedback is not an opportunity to argue with the publisher, push your points, or tell them why they're wrong. Trust us, you cannot *well, actually* your way into a book contract.

We wish this were a given, but, sadly, some folks seem to need a reminder: do not badger, harass, or insult the editors. That kind of rudeness burns bridges (with the publisher, yes, but also with the authors they work with and other publishers—bad gas travels fast in a small industry!). We know rejection doesn't feel great, but give yourself time to process, and don't take out negative reactions on the messengers.

Take whatever feedback you've been given and do something good with it. Find a new publisher who might be a better fit. Revamp your thesis. Overhaul your outline. Polish your pitch. Stay true to your ideas, of course, but treat rejections as opportunities for iteration and improvement.

Synthesizing "maybe" or "yes, but"

It seems like a publisher response should be an immediate binary—just yes or no. But sometimes proposals fall into a befuddling gray area, where the publisher wants to say yes but something's not quite right yet—maybe they need to see more details or clarity, or maybe they want to review a writing sample, or maybe they can see potential in your idea but the pitch just isn't expressing it. Some publishers will provide feedback and even work with you to develop your proposal further. Feedback can range from high-level input on your book's approach and scope to more detailed thoughts about structure, outline, audience, and even voice and tone.

If a publisher responds to you with anything other than a clear no, take advantage of the opportunity to sort out how you might get to a yes. First, reply in a timely manner. Second, if they haven't shared specific feedback on why they're not accepting the proposal *yet*, ask. Also, ask what the next steps are. If they're asking you to rethink or rework something, ask them when they want to see the revision and what happens next if they like it. This is *your* book project and *your* experience. Ask for what you need. You have (at least) our permission.

Celebrating "yes"

When your proposal is accepted, stop and don't do anything else before you *celebrate*. This is huge! Congrats! Writing a book is a big, long, messy undertaking, made a little nicer by celebrating the milestones. So go get a donut, buy yourself a new plant, or whatever sufficiently marks this joyous moment.

ACCEPTED! NOW WHAT?

When a publisher likes your pitch and wants to publish your book, they'll usually send a note of acceptance along with a preview of what to expect next. If they don't do that, you should definitely ask about what to expect. (Also, that would be a little weird; maybe make sure they're legit.) Typically, they'll want to start a conversation about the writing timeline and share a contract for your review.

Anatomy of a contract

When it comes to publishing contracts (or contracts in general, really), please read them. Most publishers aren't out to get you, but it's always good to have a thorough read-through of any legally binding documents you're about to sign.

Most of the time, contracts aren't terribly open to negotiation, but you always have the power to ask for changes, even if the answer may be no. If you have the resources to hire a lawyer for contract review, do that. If you have a lawyer in your family or friend group and you're comfortable asking for a favor, do that. If none of that kind of help or perspective is available to you (the case for most folks), here are a few big things to look out for:

- **Copyright.** The copyright for the work (a.k.a. the book) should be registered with the author's name (that's you) and the author's name *only*.
- **Royalties.** Royalty details should be unambiguous. The contract should outline what the royalty split is between author and publisher, what the payment terms are (quarterly, yearly, etc.), and how the royalties are calculated (based on net sales, for example).
- **Timelines.** Timelines for manuscript delivery, proposed book-release timing, editing deadlines, and more (or less!)

will appear in a contract. Confirm that any timelines explicitly outlined in the contract work for you—and if they don't, say so as soon as possible.

- **Warranties.** The warranties section of most contracts can look scary, but it's not. It's an assurance that you are the sole proprietor of the work you're creating (that it's your intellectual property and not borrowed or stolen from someone or somewhere else). It may also include assurances that the work is original and isn't libelous, slanderous, or plagiarized.
- **Discontinuance.** Discontinuance language may look forgettable, but take note of the details here. Often, you'll learn what happens to the rights to publish your book should it go out of print for any reason. Typically, once a book goes "out of print," the authors are allowed to terminate the existing contract and revert rights back to themselves. The important thing to ascertain regarding discontinuance is how the publisher is defining "out of print."
- **Insolvency of publisher.** Like discontinuance, language around insolvency of publisher is where you'll learn what happens to the rights to publish your book should the publisher cease to do business (or exist) for any reason.

Legal language is logical and specialized (and often dread-inducing), but not beyond your grasp. You should feel confident before signing any legal agreement. We encourage you to research the words and phrases you're not familiar with, and, when in doubt, ask questions.

Finding the right fit

You don't have to sign with the first publisher that offers you a deal. If you're shopping your proposal around and you get more than one contract offer (hell, yeah!), there's no reason you can't treat it like navigating a job offer. It's your decision and your project; you are allowed to articulate what you want and your expectations about working with a publisher.

Ask your potential publisher questions to get clarity on their editorial process and publishing logistics. You don't have to wait until you've signed a contract if you're already in promising conversations about your book pitch. Critically, you'll want to know:

- **Does the copyright live with the author or the publisher?** Usually, a publisher will handle the copyright paperwork on behalf of their authors, but the authors own their respective copyright. This is what happens at ABA.
- **Does the publisher pay a writing advance?** Large publishing houses will sometimes pay an advance, which is essentially a signing bonus offered to the author before the book is published. Even though they're paid *before* the book is published, advances must be recouped, meaning additional royalty payments are made only after the initial advance has been recouped in book sales. Advances vary wildly in amount and are generally paid in multiple installments at significant milestones in the process, such as signing the contract, delivery of a complete manuscript, and publishing. At ABA, we do not pay a writing advance, but we offer a very competitive royalty split.
- **How is the royalty split or book revenue structured?** Oh, we're so glad you asked! Publishing companies rarely share their royalty structures publicly, but we can tell you anecdotally that average author royalties from traditional publishers fall between 10 and 15 percent on hardcover sales, 5 and 8 percent on paperback sales, and up to 25 percent on ebook sales. In the interest of transparency, A Book Apart pays authors a higher percentage than the industry average to reflect our belief that publishing is a partnership.
- **What kind of promotion and marketing support does the publisher offer?** To be honest, marketing support is *wildly* inconsistent from publisher to publisher. You could get the backing of a full marketing and publicity team, or an email wishing you happy launch day and good luck. In most cases, the publisher will feature your book on their website, send a few advance reading copies to select reviewers, and issue a press release—and you may or may not be informed as to when or how these things will happen. It's up to you to ask questions and make sure your book is promoted, marketed, and sold in ways that meet your expectations. (At ABA, we

work with each author to develop a custom marketing plan that works for them and their book. More about that in Chapter 7.)

- **Do I need an agent?** Probably not. At least, it's not necessary if you're appealing to a relatively narrow or specific audience (like people who design, write, and code). Agents can be helpful for authors writing trade books, including fiction and memoirs, and for authors working with big-name publishers.

Though we didn't formally list it above, one other important thing to consider is how the publisher fit *feels*. We know locking in on a feeling or a vibe can seem nebulous at best and might be influenced by anything from how clear the communication with the publisher has been, to how supported you feel, to how the royalties are split. But we trust that you know on a gut level when an opportunity feels *right* or *not right*.

TIME TO WRITE

Now that you've put an approach together—whether that's a signed contract or a solid DIY plan—it's time to write a book.

Hey, *hey*, don't leave now. We've seen that look before. But honestly, you've gotten this far by thinking *a lot* about your book already. You've declared, at least to yourself, that you're writing a book. You've put your ideas into organized containers in the form of an outline and maybe a book proposal. Clearly, you're committed.

And sure, you *still* might be thinking, *How the heck do I even start drafting a whole entire book?* Don't worry, we've got you— that's our next stop!

4 CLEANING YOUR WHOLE HOUSE, OR, DRAFTING

❝ I love writing projects. They concentrate the highest number of crippling insecurities over the longest period of time possible.
—ETHAN MARCOTTE (http://bkaprt.com/ysw40/04-01/)

OUR FIRST ORDER OF BUSINESS is obliterating the lie that writing is a process of mechanically producing pages of text until you've filled your book. Ha ha, who's responsible for this garbage nonsense? Was it Hemingway? We bet it was Hemingway. Screw that guy.

Truth: writing mostly involves staring out a window for a really long time, punctuated by:

- doomscrolling Twitter
- watching TikToks of dogs sitting on cats
- tamping down pangs of self-doubt
- doing laundry
- unloading the dishwasher
- more self-doubt
- vacuuming? vacuuming might help
- when was the last time we cleaned the sink
- is it just us, or are these windows, like, *really* dirty

The actual typing of words into a computer is a really, *really* tiny part of the overall process, and many authors will prioritize quite a lot of other tasks (see list) when they are feeling anxious about the typing. Most authors will admit that writing is just hard: it's hard to keep one's butt in a chair (or feet on a floor, or legs in a hammock, we don't know your furniture arrangement), it's hard to stay motivated (especially in this, the worst timeline), and it's hard to find time to write. It's so, so hard to keep faith in oneself and one's work. Writing takes courage and perseverance and patience and privilege.

Writing is also a deeply personal process, one that can't be prescribed with any guarantees. There is no one right way to *write a book*. Some people are very linear thinkers, writing everything in the order dictated by their outline. Other people jump around, writing chunks wherever the mood strikes them and filling in connective tissue later. Most of us probably fall somewhere in the smudgy area between those approaches. Work on your book in whatever way makes the most sense to you.

YOUR BRAIN ON WRITING

As much as we like to joke (or ardently believe) that writing is a mystical process that somehow just *happens*, science actually does have some insight here. In 1980, researchers John R. Hayes and Linda Flower articulated the human brain's writing process across three phases (**FIG 4.1**):

1. **Planning** is the first phase and is exactly what it sounds like. It has three subprocesses:
    a) **Generating**, or "retrieving information relevant to the writing task from long-term memory"—that is, coming up with ideas
    b) **Organizing**, or arranging those ideas into a logical presentation order, maybe by composing an outline (which we discussed in Chapter 2)
    c) **Goal-setting**, or identifying your criteria for completion

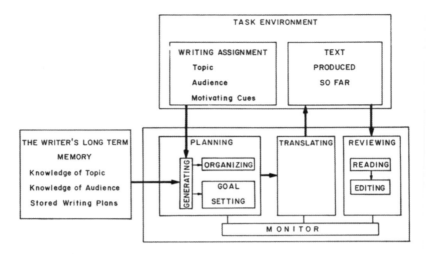

TASK ENVIRONMENT

WRITING ASSIGNMENT	TEXT
Topic	PRODUCED
Audience	SO FAR
Motivating Cues	

THE WRITER'S LONG TERM MEMORY
Knowledge of Topic
Knowledge of Audience
Stored Writing Plans

PLANNING — GENERATING — ORGANIZING — GOAL SETTING

TRANSLATING

REVIEWING — READING — EDITING

MONITOR

FIG 4.1: The act of writing pushes our brains through three phases—planning, translating, and reviewing—while simultaneously analyzing our stored knowledge, our writing assignment, and the text we're producing. Isn't writing magical? (http://bkaprt.com/ysw40/04-02/, PDF)

- -

2. **Translating**, the second phase, is what we might call the writing itself: you are translating your ideas into written language, on the page or on the screen, to communicate with external readers.

3. **Reviewing**, the third phase, is for "improving the quality of the text produced by the translating process...by detecting and correcting weaknesses in the text with respect to language conventions and accuracy of meaning, and by evaluating the extent to which the text accomplishes the writer's goals." Translation: editing (which we'll be discussing in Chapter 5). This phase actually has two subprocesses:

   a) **Reading** what you've written

   b) **Editing** what you've just read

You certainly don't need to understand this process in order to write. But we find it helps to recognize that the writing process isn't inscrutable—in fact, it's a pretty hardwired, standardized procedure. Our brains all follow this same script,

LAWFUL GOOD	NEUTRAL GOOD	CHAOTIC GOOD
Alphabetical digital filing system of color-coded folders, docs, and spreadsheets for each project	A folder or document each for interviews, research, and the draft itself, as well as images and media	One "super Google doc" with the draft at the top and everything else below
LAWFUL NEUTRAL	TRUE NEUTRAL	CHAOTIC NEUTRAL
Scrivener or some sort of program for organizing notes	One document for drafting, one document for notes and research	Sticky notes Sticky notes everywhere
LAWFUL EVIL	NEUTRAL EVIL	CHAOTIC EVIL
Notes app with the internet turned off to avoid distraction	Research and write draft by hand and then transfer to computer	Write directly into the CMS

FIG 4.2: Choose your writing workflow alignment. (Based on http://bkaprt.com/ysw40/04-03/)

even if our individual tactics for generating, organizing, and translating vary widely.

At the start of your drafting journey, do a little bit of self-reflection about the kind of writer you are—not your style or voice, but your way of working. We talked about this a little bit when it came to outlines, but now we're in the thick of it: Are you a planner? An iterator? A messy witch who lives for drama (**FIG 4.2**)? Your drafting process can take any shape or approach, but we recommend going with the flow of your own current—don't create extra friction at the start by trying to emulate schedules or approaches that aren't your own. There are plenty of other hurdles ahead.

THE TYRANNY OF TIME

The single biggest obstacle to actually writing a book is, simply, time. We've lost many would-be authors to sudden, unexpected demands on their time, like new projects, job upheaval, fluctuations in living arrangements, caregiving challenges, unexpected illnesses, and constitutional crises.

Living through late-stage capitalism aside, many folks are often waiting for more ideal circumstances to begin their big project—but, as writer Ijeoma Oluo put it, there's never a *good* time to write:

> *Trust me when I say this: every stage of life is a shitshow. There is no time in your career that is a "better time" to start writing. There is no time in your relationship that is a "better time" to start writing. There is no time in your kid's development that is a "better time" for you to start writing. There are only bad times and impossible times. During the impossible times, it just won't get done. During the bad times, it won't want to get done, but it can still get done. A "good" time doesn't come around. (http://bkaprt.com/ysw40/04-04/)*

One key to enabling writing during "the bad times" is setting boundaries—and having the support in one's life to enforce them. First, set boundaries with yourself: recognize that writing a book is *work* and takes *time*. The only way it's going to get done is if you give it the same gravity that you'd give to any paid project. Next, communicate your boundaries clearly to the other people in your life and ask for their support in guarding them. Your managers and direct reports, your partners, your children, your friends—if they have the potential to interrupt or consume your time, figure out how to enlist their help in minimizing that potential.

Boundaries don't mean there won't be times when you miss a deadline, skip a writing session, or pause your research, but you're a lot more likely to find success in getting the draft done with them in place.

Many authors (past and present) have, to put it lightly, *help* in managing their boundaries, particularly around financial, familial, and social obligations—privilege allows them to dedicate themselves fully to their projects. The rest of us have to get more creative (and usually end up more depleted from the effort).

Let's be clear: it's deeply unfair that we can't take the time we need to usher our ideas into the world. Most of us already have to beg, borrow, and steal time just to keep the lights on. And now that you have an idea for a book—a difficult pursuit even under ideal circumstances—you somehow have to find time to make it happen.

Some authors can afford to take time off from bill-paying work to focus on writing. Others have employers who offer sabbaticals or generous leave policies as a benefit. Still others are able to use business hours to write, since, after all, their success and reputation as an expert reflects positively on their employers. (This is a trade-off: if you want support from your employer, you'll owe them good press; if they want control of your content, they'll owe you time.)

If you can't get sponsored, pause your projects, or take a sabbatical, you'll have to do what authors since time immemorial have done: write before breakfast, during lunch breaks, in your evenings, and on your weekends. Take long weekends and barricade yourself in a quiet space with no other responsibilities (if you can afford it, hotel rooms work wonders). Public libraries are also a (free) font of quiet space. Shut out the world, turn up those lo-fi chill beats, and get as much done as you can before you're forced to return to your regularly scheduled life.

Ultimately, be realistic about when and how you can get your writing done. Recognize the range of commitment and accountability that's accessible to you, and plan accordingly.

Managing your schedule

Finding time is one thing; managing it is a different beast entirely. The first thing to do is determine your pace: how much do you need to write, and how much time do you have to write it?

A standard A Book Apart book, for example, is about 35,000 words. (For reference, the average novel is about 80,000-100,000 words; blog posts are generally between 400 and 2,000 words.) Our authors usually complete their first drafts in about four months, which shakes out to writing about 8,750 words a month, or just over 2,000 words a week.

You can estimate your workload (and then gauge your progress) by averaging your word count across your drafting timeline, but you don't necessarily have to stick to that pace. In fact, count on *not*: you may draft an entire chapter in just a few days, then go several weeks without writing at all. Treat this math as a planning tool, and grant yourself some grace in the execution. (And remember: It's always going to take longer than you think. *Always*.)

A few other recommendations for planning your drafting (and sticking to it):

- **Break your book into chunks.** "Writing the book" is way too big to be realistic or sustainable when sitting down to write. Instead, take on smaller, more achievable chunks during any given writing session. Focus on a single chapter or section, a certain number of words, or a specific question to answer through research.
- **Timebox your writing.** Writing for eight straight hours is not...a thing (as we hope we've established by now). But you can get a lot done in just a few hours, if those hours are respected, as designer and content strategist Scott Kubie recommends in *Writing for Designers*: "Blocking off time on your calendar to write—and protecting that time against meetings and interruptions—is a good start, and more than many writers are able to pull off." (We keep trying!)
- **Regularly review your progress.** Whether you're measuring word count or not, you should regularly check what you've drafted against the timeline or plan you've made. If you're halfway through your proposed draft timeline, but you don't feel halfway done with the manuscript, that's a good moment to reassess your plan.
- **Get external accountability.** If you're working with an editor, they may have regular check-ins with you or deadlines for each chapter. If not, you may want to connect with a community (e.g., a writing group, a Slack channel, a hashtag)

that can provide accountability. That accountability doesn't have to be other writers—you may only need a place to post "I hit my goal!" or "Anyone have any recommendations for shutting out distractions?"

If you feel like you're falling behind on your writing, take several calming breaths (trust us, no book was ever improved by panic), and then think about what adjustments you could make: maybe you need to slow your pace, reduce your word count, lengthen your sprints, or call in a new accountability partner (pick someone who really loves spreadsheets). If you have an editor, talk to them immediately—it's literally their job to help you get your draft drafted, and the sooner you tell them where you're struggling, the sooner they can help you get back on track.

Life happens, and big projects don't always unfold with the speed and elegance we wish they would. Our ultimate advice here: work diligently, but be gentle with yourself.

KEEPING MOMENTUM

Now that you've sorted out your plan for getting the writing done, well—there's really nothing else you can do to procrastinate (unless you haven't finished your laundry yet). You actually have to write now. To quote our dogs when they get a bath, *This is the worst thing that's ever happened.* But there are a few steps you can take to minimize obstacles and keep the words flowing as much as possible.

Something from nothing

If the blinking cursor in a sea of digital white grinds your writing gears to a halt, know that you're far from alone. Many authors find the blank page to be an immediate inspiration-killer (FIG 4.3).

Our advice here is simple: don't start from a blank page. Rather than trying to force words to materialize from nothing-

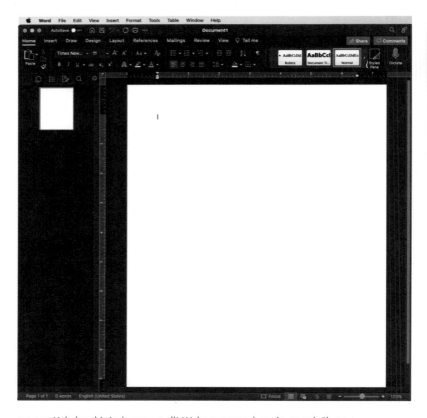

FIG 4.3: Hahaha, this isn't scary at all! We're not scared, *you're* scared. Shut up.

ness, build from your outline, your notes, your research, or any other material that's been part of your preparation thus far.

An outline is a particularly great candidate for jump-starting your drafting. Go to any part of it and add a detail: another idea, an explanatory sentence, a secondary example, even a placeholder, like "talk to Malaika about this" or "insert statistics here" or "remember that article about algorithmic bias."

Keep doing this until you run out of steam—fiddle with one bullet or section, then move on to another. You may find you've accidentally turned fragments into sentences and sentences into whole paragraphs. It breaks the spell of pressure and formality that "writing a book" can sometimes cast.

If outlines aren't your thing, maybe slide decks are. Many tech professionals deliver conference talks and workshops before they ever decide to write a book. David Dylan Thomas told us a slide deck was his first stop when he started drafting *Design for Cognitive Bias*:

> *The first draft was easy for me, because I just opened up the deck for my talk and wrote down each slide, one at a time. The hard part was after that, because I realized I had to structure it differently to work as a book. Stories that you tell in front of an audience don't sound the same when written down, so there was a lot of adaptation.*

A more familiar format can help you ease into the newness of long-form writing. And easing in is sometimes the key with drafting, as Thomas continued:

> *Start with whatever it is you already know how to do. It can be intimidating to think about the form of the book, its structure, its logistics. But a book is just a vessel. Get the ideas down first—make it a podcast, make it a Trello board, make it a conversation. However you are comfortable processing ideas, let that be your first step.*

If you still find yourself overwhelmed by the enormity of the drafting task, keep in mind that it's merely one part of the overall process. With all the rounds of drafting and editing ahead of you, your first take will hardly resemble the final product, so don't put undue pressure on yourself to make it perfect. Write a *terrible* first draft. They're the best.

Getting unstuck

No matter how much momentum you generate at the start, or how careful you are in planning your work or managing your time, you will encounter moments when the writing feels like pulling teeth. Most writers find that their drafting energy naturally ebbs and flows. Sometimes those ebbs are simply clues to take a break, but other times you may want to investigate the source of the resistance. Is it external—work stress, a health issue, exhaustion—or is it coming from inside the book?

Ask yourself a few questions to diagnose the problem:

- **Are you missing information?** It's tough to move the writing forward if you're not certain of what you want to say. Go back to your prep materials: review your notes, reread your research, look for new sources. Sometimes a fresh anecdote or different example can open up an unexpected avenue of inquiry.
- **Are you bored, in a rut, or spinning your wheels?** Maybe you have all the information, but you haven't spent enough time digesting it. Reexamine the questions you're asking, the answers you're providing, and your assumptions underlying both. Try changing your framing, asking different questions, or—as a mental exercise—arguing the opposite. Change lenses, change scale, or change angles until you find a new handhold.
- **Are you writing the right thing?** If you find yourself repeatedly avoiding a particular section, it might be that you need to dig in harder—but it might also be your book telling you to choose a different path. For example, when Lisa Maria was drafting *Everyday Information Architecture*, she had planned for a chapter all about content modeling—but every time she sat down to write it, nothing happened. After every other chapter had been written, she finally had to admit the topic just wasn't in her. And thank goodness for that resistance—by giving herself permission to *not* write the chapter, she was able to focus on the chapters in front of her, and the book coalesced into a tighter, stronger narrative.
- **Are you hungry?** Or thirsty? Have you moved your body today? Have you rested it enough? We're all looking forward to the day we can upload our consciousnesses into machines or become sentient ether, but, until then, bodies need to be taken care of. For maximum mental clarity, make sure to tend to your physical needs!

If you've tried every possible tactic to get the words flowing and you're still stuck, try taking a break. Time and distance can heal a lot of perceived writing wounds, and our brains need breathing room—especially if you're untangling a particularly complex conceptual problem or trying to synthesize a large body of research. Writing takes time, and, as we know, precious little of that time is spent on wordcraft.

Staying focused

A final recommendation for your drafting: try not to edit yourself as you go. While everyone's process is different, and some folks do find it helpful to revise freshly minted words, it's a good idea to keep your brain in a generative mode rather than a critical one.

Your goal in the drafting phase is to get as many words on the page as possible. You should aim for big-picture thinking, conceptual clarity, logical order, and narrative structure. If you slip into editing mode too early, you could end up spending your time and energy fine-tuning details—and you don't even know if those details will be sticking around for later drafts.

If you're less prone to self-editing but find yourself getting distracted by endless tangents, excess narrative details, or over-wrought explanations, you may find it helpful to maintain a separate file as a sort of holding pen for wayward ideas. Not only will it help you keep your manuscript a little more focused in the moment, but you'll also have it as a resource later in the process: those extraneous thoughts can become fodder for supporting blog posts and other marketing efforts after launch.

Another way of diverting relevant-but-extra book material is to include a section for additional resources in the back of the book. Collecting resources in a dedicated place means you can focus on your most meaningful content in the actual text rather than trying to cover every possible related concept. It will also give readers who are deeply interested in your topic an immediate next step (or ten).

Of course, in order to provide such a list of resources—or do any drafting at all, really—you'll need to have done something we've only hinted at thus far: research.

CONDUCTING RESEARCH

Before and during your drafting, you'll have to do some research. Solid research in your book shows you've been paying attention to your industry and will earn you the respect of those you cite. While you've already done some initial research—it's hard to put together a book outline or proposal without having, you know, read other books—you'll want to spend some time doing more focused research to support specific aspects of your topic.

Your sources can come from many places: books, blog posts, academic papers, conference talks, podcasts, tweets, anecdotes from coworkers, your own experiences, and more. Every book has some measure of research, but your topic, your book's style, and your approach to writing will dictate how much and what kind.

Incorporating research

Those same factors also affect how you incorporate your research into your book—but we can suggest a few basic principles:

- **Synthesize and build.** Doing research is one thing; integrating it with your own ideas is quite another. First, make sure you understand what's being said in the original source, and identify the most important points for your readers. Then, share the research with your readers (by quoting or paraphrasing it) while articulating the main takeaway and connecting it to your own insights, advice, or recommendations.
- **Support your ideas, but let them lead.** Citing other resources is an excellent practice that can lend your writing authority. But don't get so focused on calling on experts that you forget to tell readers what *you* think! Readers want to hear your take on the topic, not just a survey of studies.
- **Use direct quotations when the language matters.** Generally, you want to directly quote someone when they've said something in an original, compelling way—that is, *how* they've said it lends meaning. If *what* they've said is important, but they've said it very neutrally (or awkwardly),

paraphrase it: restate the idea in your own way while giving them credit for the concept.

- **Choose primary sources when possible.** Sometimes we read about a study or a report via an article or book—for example, a *FastCompany* article might reference a Pew study, or a blog post might discuss data released by Instagram. Rather than citing the article or the blog post in these cases, cite the original data instead—your interpretation of the source material is more direct and credible than your interpretation of someone else's interpretation.
- **Cite sources clearly.** Most anything that didn't originate in your own head—anecdotes, direct quotations, paraphrases, statistics—requires a citation, a way of pointing readers to the source material. Check with your publisher, if you're working with one, to see if they have a preferred method for citations. At minimum, you should include the source's title, the author's name, and a link to the original source, not only to provide credit but also to provide context and additional paths of research for your readers.

Properly incorporating your research and crediting your sources is respectful, responsible, and just plain good manners. You are in conversation with everyone in the industry who has written before you, and everyone who will write after you—so act like it. Give credit where it's due. Build on others' ideas, just as future authors will build on yours!

Diverse and inclusive sources

Which brings us to a critical point: while you're properly acknowledging those who paved the way for your thinking, remember that the voices of the past are more likely to be white, male, cis, straight, and able-bodied. This is not because they had the best ideas at the time, but because they were more likely (and are *still* more likely) to be given access to public platforms.

When we look to build on the work that's come before us, we must also be thinking about how our contributions will shape the future. If we want to see more diversity of voices in our industry (and in others), if we want to believe that the future is more equitable, then we have to start now, in what *we* write. This means actively choosing to amplify voices from communities that are marginalized in our industry.

Do some self-interrogation about your information sources, your processes for seeking out new information, and the media you consume *as a matter of course*. Examine what kind of spaces you're immersed in and where there might be opportunity to diversify. Ask yourself:

- Whom do you follow on social media?
- Who has written the technical books on your shelves?
- Who has written the blog posts you read?
- Who's in the leadership of the companies you pay attention to?
- Who's on stage at the conferences you attend?
- When you participate in industry discussions, whom do you listen to?
- When you share other people's work (including retweets), whose work are you sharing?
- Who's following you?

And you might ask the opposite of all of those questions too: whom *aren't* you listening to? Whose work *aren't* you sharing? Whom *aren't* you following? Where do you see room for broadening your exposure to a variety of voices?

How many people from groups that have historically been excluded in countries like the United States (**FIG 4.4**) do you count among your sources? Among your professional circles? Among your friends? If you find you have room for improvement (and most of us do), start making changes before you even begin writing: identify new voices, follow new people (in both your professional and personal spaces), and ask around for connections and introductions. These sources are out there, and it is incumbent on you to include them.

Authors who aren't already intentional about cultivating diverse professional circles may find these steps challenging. Adding in representative sources *after* they've done the bulk of their own thinking will feel half-hearted and extraneous— because it is.

IDENTITY	HISTORICALLY INCLUDED GROUPS	HISTORICALLY EXCLUDED GROUPS
Race, skin color, ethnicity	White	Black, Indigenous, and other people of color
Gender	Men	Women, transgender, nonbinary, gender-nonconforming
Socioeconomic class	Owning class, middle class	Poor, working class, unhoused
Education	Formally educated	Informally or alternatively educated
Employment	Managers, faculty, full-time employees	Retail, clerical, students, unemployed/underemployed
Religion	Protestant Christians	Muslims, Jews, other non-Christians, and Catholics
Age	Young adults, adults	Elders, children
Sexual orientation	Heterosexuals	Gay, lesbian, bisexual, transgender, queer, intersex, asexual
Physical or mental ability	Able-bodied	Physically or mentally disabled, neurodivergent, chronically ill
Immigrant status	Citizens, native-born	Immigrants, undocumented
Spoken language	English	English as a second language, non-English-speaking

FIG 4.4: For every facet of identity in a country like the United States, some groups of people are given more societal power, while others are given less.

This limitation can happen to anyone, not only authors of dominant-group identities, because we consciously and unconsciously absorb so many biases from the surrounding society (http://bkaprt.com/ysw40/04-05/). When we first start out in the tech industry, it's very easy to follow only the ideas of whoever seems loudest or most popular, even if those voices are homogenous, flawed, or even harmful. But we don't have to reinforce those voices in new work: we can look for new heroes, in all disciplines, from wider walks of life.

A new book is an opportunity to broaden horizons—both yours and those of your readers—to open the gates wider and bring more people in to the wonderful world of web work.

ARE WE THERE YET?

A question first-time authors often ask is, "How do I know when my draft is done?"

Your first draft is done when it's done. This sounds silly, but we mean it literally: Is it complete? The entire manuscript has to be written! It shouldn't feel final, but it should feel whole. If it's still got "TK" and "note to self: write more about this" strewn about like glitter, well, maybe keep writing a little more.

There's a second, more strategic way to know when the draft is drafted: when you recognize that you've taken it as far as you can *on your own*. Even if you feel like there's a lot more work to do—and you will, because it's a bad first draft!—there will come a point where you're sick of your own brain and your own eyes looking at your own words. You'll start to feel hemmed in by the limits of your own perspective. Your draft is done when you're ready—nay, *hungry*—for feedback.

And when you've reached that point, well, there be dragons. The editing process is every bit as hairy as the drafting process, and not for the faint of heart. But, if you've made it this far, we've got faith in you. Press on into the wild lands of editing.

5 THE EDITING PROCESS

> *The secret to editing your work is simple: you need to become its reader instead of its writer.*
> —ZADIE SMITH

THE MOMENT YOU FINISH that first draft, you may be tempted to break out the champagne and swear off writing forever. And for sure, we support celebrating—you've just hit a huge milestone! But you're certainly not done with writing, not by a long shot. (Our condolences.)

Now we begin the editing process, which exists specifically to give your writing the time and attention it needs to truly bloom. Editing is not just about fixing spelling (though you will, at some point, fix spelling); it's a chance to critically assess what you've written and improve it for your audience. Think of it as iterating—trying out different words, different formats, and different framings to more effectively convey the ideas at the heart of your manuscript.

You want to make sure your ideas will actually land with your audience. Your first attempt at explaining an idea is almost never the best version of that explanation—you may go off on tangents, backtrack to share additional history or context, overexplain steps that aren't important, or rush through steps that are. Editing helps ensure that you're choosing the *best* way to communicate your ideas, not just the *first* way.

And, maybe more important, editing is an opportunity to step back from what was likely an intense, emotional, and exhausting drafting process. During the drafting process, you're often a little bit in love with your ideas (or completely disgusted with them, or both), which is understandable—you're passionate about your topic. That's why you're writing a book! Passion is a wonderful motivator, but it's not always the most clear-eyed. And you want a little clarity before you hit the presses.

Whether you're editing yourself or working with an entire editorial team, it's worth taking the time and effort to make your ideas truly shine.

EDITING YOURSELF

Before you share your work with friends, editors, or other readers, give yourself a break—preferably a few weeks, but even a few days away from the draft will help. When you come back to it, read it slowly and carefully, from beginning to end, with as distanced an eye as you can possibly give it. You'll catch typos, of course, but also garbled sentences, confusing explanations, unintentional repetition, and incomplete thoughts—that's how first drafts go!

If you haven't done any formal editing before, it might feel like rereading your manuscript to "fix everything" is a tall order. It is! Which is why we recommend thinking about revisions across three broad categories: voice and tone, language and inclusivity, and craft and presentation.

Voice and tone

Spend some time noticing your voice so you know what you're editing for. When we say *voice*, we mean how you sound to your reader: your style, your diction, your level of formality, your word choice, your sentence length, and all manner of other personal quirks that show up in your writing.

Maybe you're very direct and dislike lengthy descriptions. Maybe you prefer colorful adjectives and lively examples. Maybe you're wordy and prone to repetition, but tell a great story. One of the authors of this book sprinkles in semicolons and em dashes like she's salting caramel, and she will not apologize for it.

Your *tone* reflects your voice, but shifts depending on immediate context. You always sound like you, but you might be more instructive and patient when explaining a difficult concept, or more lighthearted when relaying a funny anecdote.

Our recommendations for editing for voice and tone:

- **Be conversational.** If you're struggling to find your own voice, try writing the way you talk. Think about how you sound when you explain your topic to a friend in a casual conversation: you're informal, you use contractions, and you probably make little jokes. You don't say "ceased daily operating hours" when you mean "closed"—you use plain language to make sure your friend is following along, no matter their background. You pause for your friend to respond and ask questions (which becomes white space and section divisions in writing). A conversational tone makes a book—even a technical one—easier to approach and understand than one steeped in jargon, formality, and dense paragraphs.
- **Be clear.** Readers want to hear your unique voice, but not at the expense of clear communication. In a first draft, err on the side of too much explanation, boring headings, and fewer jokes; you can always make things fancier or funnier once you're certain your message is being received.
- **Be practical.** At A Book Apart, we're pretty focused on practicality—what the reader can do *right now* to become a better web practitioner. This action-driven approach may not be true for every publisher or every style of book, but it's never a bad idea to ask yourself what you want the reader to do with the information you're presenting. Giving readers immediate, pragmatic recommendations will help them get as much value from your ideas as possible.

- **Be responsible.** *Active voice* is writing where you can tell who is responsible for the action in a sentence, while *passive voice* hides the responsibility. Consider "Optimize your images" (active voice) versus "Images should be optimized" (passive voice): in the active sentence, the reader is responsible for optimizing images, while in the passive sentence, the responsibility is on the images to miraculously optimize themselves. Not only does passive voice make the writing sound weak, but the lack of responsibility can create actual harm (http://bkaprt.com/ysw40/05-01/). Here's our best tip: reread your sentence, and if you can successfully add the phrase "by zombies" to the end—*ding ding ding!*—that's a passive sentence, bay-bee. ("Images should be optimized *by zombies*" has some spoopy implications for web performance.)

But our most crucial advice? *Be yourself.* You don't need to sound a certain way, say certain things, or write in any voice other than your own to write a good book. Lean into the styles, experiences, and perspectives that make you *you* and your book *yours*.

Of course, it can be difficult to feel confident in your voice if you don't have a lot of writing experience, and even more so if you have an identity that has been marginalized by the tech and publishing industries. Author David Dylan Thomas told us:

> Some people think that if you're going to write a talk or a book, you have to put on a different persona. This is especially true for Black folks, who often think they have to use a white voice in order to give a talk or write a book. If I want to hear a white voice, there's no shortage—that market's been cornered. But I have nowhere else I can go to hear you.

Readers want to hear what *you* have to say. Showing up as yourself, as much as you can, contributes to authentic, compelling writing.

Language and inclusivity

We love to say that language is a playground—but that doesn't mean it's without guidelines for fair play. Words carry tremendous power, and how we choose to wield that power—to bring readers in or shut them out—should be at the forefront of every writer's practice.

You should have power dynamics in mind as you draft, but editing is another shot at examining and rebalancing those dynamics. Use the editing process to root out implicit biases, cognitive fallacies, and language that may be (however unintentionally) racist, sexist, ableist, classist, or dehumanizing. If you don't deliberately write and edit *against* unconscious bias, you will be deliberately allowing it in, because that's how society works. Good editors incorporate this awareness into their work, and you should too.

To that end, here are some recommendations for editing your language:

- **Be inclusive.** Use gender-neutral language and avoid unnecessary binaries; we stan the third-person singular pronoun *they*. We also try to avoid ableist language (words like *crazy*, *blind*, and *lame*), language derived from violence and conflict (like *trigger* and *marching orders*), and language that reinforces harmful dichotomies (like associating *white* with good and *black* with evil). Don't punch down; don't make jokes or use metaphors that represent real points of pain for people. Just as we can't control how people use a website, we can't control the experiences readers bring to our books.
- **Avoid using idioms if you don't know their origin.** Not only are idioms difficult to translate (don't you want your book to have global relevance?), but many idioms in English also have racist origins. Many phrases commonly used in American business contexts (like "cakewalk," "cargo cult," "off the reservation," etc.) have colonialist foundations. Do your research!
- **Watch your assumptions.** Just as we sometimes forget that our users don't all have the latest iPhone and perfect bandwidth, we sometimes forget that our readers come from

incredibly diverse backgrounds that don't match our own. Even within our target audiences, our readers may have much less (or more) formal education than ourselves, may be much older or younger than we expect, or may live in countries or regions that we haven't considered.

- **Be careful with pop culture references.** Readers will have varied interests and cultural touchstones. That's not to say you shouldn't reference the media you consume—Lisa Maria lost track of how many anime titles she mentioned in *Everyday Information Architecture,* so she's really not one to talk here—but ask yourself what will happen if a reader doesn't get your reference. Use pop culture references sparingly, and only in contexts where the reference could be missed or ignored with no detriment to the surrounding material.

If you're going to take the time to write an entire book, why not write it as thoughtfully and inclusively as you can? Why not make it as relevant and empowering to as many readers as possible?

Craft and presentation

Craft refers to the actual construction of the text—the writing itself and your skill in wielding it. Improving your craft means finessing your presentation (e.g., tightening sentences, creating flow) and ending up with a book that doesn't just share your ideas, but sings them.

We don't want to get into the weeds about how to write (there are a million books about improving your craft out there—see the Resources section), but we can offer a few tips and tricks for shining up your draft:

- **Take down your scaffolding.** Often in writing a first draft, we ramble around a bit to discover what we truly want to say. We call that rambling *scaffolding*—the writing you do to get to the *real* writing. It may be perfectly good content, but it may also distract from the narrative, or simply not necessary. Scaffolding shows up most often in introductory sections, where authors tend to rev their conceptual engines before diving into a topic. If you learn to recognize these bits of written scaffolding and then remove them (let them happen! Just don't keep them forever), you'll strengthen your writing considerably.

- **Reduce repetition.** First drafts are riddled with repetition. We repeat ourselves because we want to get a point across, or because we were trying to find the best way to say something, or because the drafting process is a hopeless ball of spaghetti—and the more you've moved sections around in your manuscript, the more likely you've accidentally copied and copied and pasted. Make sure you're reiterating your ideas (to help readers learn and remember!) without duplicating content.
- **Add segues.** Segues—connecting material at the beginnings and endings of chapters and sections—help create narrative engagement, bridge ideas, set reader expectations, and reiterate key takeaways. These on- and off-ramps not only help you layer your lessons and improve flow, but also help readers better understand the material.
- **Define your terms.** Define jargon and spell out acronyms on their first mention; don't assume your readers will know what everything means. And jargon doesn't just mean technobabble—anything that requires specialized knowledge is jargon to someone without that knowledge. If you're using terms of your own creation, make sure you use them consistently throughout the book to avoid confusion.
- **Vary your methods.** Just because you're writing a book doesn't mean it's a nonstop river of prose: white space, bulleted lists, tables, and images (which we'll talk about in a moment) provide visual variety in your manuscript, and may communicate your content more effectively than long, wordy paragraphs.

As a bonus, editing will not only improve your book, it will also improve your writing skills generally. As you examine your craft with a critical eye, you'll become more aware of your writing's strengths and weaknesses, and will learn stronger ways of expressing yourself the next time around.

TIDYING UP

Once you've conducted an initial review of your draft to your satisfaction, you'll want to take a second pass with an eye toward the scariest thing of all: letting other people see your work. Whether you're preparing to share it with your partner, your coworker, or your editorial team, make sure the document itself is ready for someone else's eyes. It's like vacuuming dog hair off the sofa before company comes over.

Images

If your book has images, make sure they're as ready for readers as your words are. At ABA, we most often see screenshots of websites used to support the text, but our authors also use charts, diagrams, illustrations, spreadsheets, graphs, tables, and personal and stock photography to round out their work. A few tips for working with imagery:

- **Choose images that add meaning.** Choose images that expand on your words; avoid images that don't contribute additional meaning. We often see GIFs in blog posts, where reader expectations run short, snappy, and meme-hungry; technical books do better with purposeful imagery that elucidates the text.
- **Include context.** Just as the images should build on your text, your text should explain the images. Captions, in particular, can describe what the reader is seeing, and offer your interpretation of the image. In addition, if your book will be available digitally, each image will need alt text; write a clear, brief explanation of the image's meaning, not just a description of its content. As information architect Anne Gibson puts it: "Ask yourself, 'If I couldn't use an image, what text would I put in its place?' to help decide what makes the most sense" (http://bkaprt.com/ysw40/05-02/).
- **Get permission.** If you didn't make an image yourself, you'll need to know where it came from and whether you can include it in your book. Fair-use guidelines can be a bit

ambiguous, so do your due diligence to identify ownership and any terms and conditions for use (and don't break any non-disclosure agreements you may have signed). Screenshots of public websites are typically considered fair use for non-commercial purposes, but you'll need to obtain legal permission to use proprietary charts, professional photography, content behind paywalls, comics, and film and television stills—which can be expensive, or even unavailable. Sorry if you had your heart set on a *Schitt's Creek* GIF.

- **Consider diversity here, too.** Just as with your research, your images should draw on the amazing breadth of examples available to us in the tech industry. If you're using website screenshots, choose sites that represent a variety of industries and organizations. If you're using photography or illustrations of people, make sure they represent the diversity of your readers.

Whatever images you choose, we recommend staying organized as you work (just as we discussed with research materials). It is way too easy to screenshot with wild abandon when you're focused on drafting—and rounding up duplicate, damaged, and missing images come production time is no picnic. Instead, try to store them by chapter, and name the files descriptively as you go.

Formatting

We don't want you to get hung up on nitty-gritty formatting details—there's plenty of time to fix fonts later. That said, there are a few minor formatting considerations to implement for the sake of your first readers:

- **Choose the right platform.** Regardless of whether you wrote your first draft in Microsoft Word, Google Docs, Scrivener, or GitHub (we've seen it), consider which platform works best for whomever you're sharing your draft with. If they expect to leave comments in the document itself, opt for a system that enables that. If they don't want tracked changes interfering with their reading, cast off a PDF or other format that keeps the reading experience simple. Additionally, if you're working with a publishing house and they've given you a manuscript template, do your best to adhere to its formats and styles.

- **Keep it legible.** If you don't have a publisher's template to follow, then the visual formatting is entirely up to you. We are not here to recommend fonts, but, you know, now's probably not the time to set your document in Papyrus. Make sure that the text is easy to read and that you're using white space to create meaningful divisions—for instance, start new chapters on new pages, make sure paragraphs don't run into one another, and apply only one style of visual emphasis at a time.
- **Manage your heading hierarchy.** Much like applying heading elements on a web page, your chapter titles, section titles, and subsection titles should be styled consistently to convey their relative importance. The main reason for this is conceptual clarity: if an editor or reviewer can't tell when a topic is nested within a larger topic, they may misinterpret your writing and make recommendations that aren't aligned with your intentions. Remember, ABC: Always Be Cbuilding information hierarchies.

One final note: if you're working with a publisher, they likely have their own house style guide and will apply it to your document without mercy—another reason not to get hung up on fonts, formats, indents, and spelling at this stage. Just make sure your manuscript is clear and accessible, and save your energy for the rest of the editing process.

Crossing *t*'s and dotting *i*'s

The easier it is for your editors, friends, or reviewers to read your manuscript (without getting distracted by errors and inconsistencies), the more easily they can focus on providing the feedback you crave. Let's make sure your draft is as buttoned-up as it can possibly be, through the cunning use of checklists:

- Is your draft in the format or template your reviewers want?
- Does your document have a title page and table of contents?
- Have you finished the writing? Have you left in any placeholders? Are there any areas you meant to return to but forgot?
- Are your chapters and sections clearly divided and labeled?
- Did you write an introductory and concluding segue for each chapter?
- Do you have all the necessary links, references, and images in the document? If not, do you have placeholder text that will give your editors the information they need to assess those elements?
- Did you close out any changes you might have tracked in the document? Did you remove any completed notes to yourself?
- Did you read back everything you wrote, check for typos and errors, and complete at least one pass of self-editing?

Wait, you did? All that? Already? Look at you go! Your draft is ready to start accepting feedback.

PEER REVIEWS

It's a great idea to have other people read your draft: they can provide the kind of objectivity that you—no matter how brilliant and attractive you are—cannot provide for yourself. At ABA, we recommend that authors share their first draft with a trusted colleague or two, prior to beginning the formal editing process. If you are not working with an editor, this is still a good time to gather feedback—after your initial self-edit, but before more rigorous rounds of review.

A *peer review*, as we call it, is not exactly an edit (because the reviewer isn't reading for the same considerations that an editor would be), but rather an opportunity to hear gut reactions and conceptual feedback from a fellow professional in your industry. Think of it like a round of prototype testing.

Whom to ask

When thinking about who can provide you with a good peer review, consider people who:

- **You know and trust:** Reach out to people who have been there for you professionally. They might be colleagues, friends, even partners. But more than that, they should be people whose opinions you value, and who you trust to give you constructive, well-reasoned criticism.
- **Are reliable and available:** Make sure your reviewers have time to read, collect their thoughts, and communicate the feedback to you. Two or three weeks is a good time frame for turnaround; if you know your reviewer will be managing their own project deadlines or life events during those weeks, ask someone else. A stressed, last-minute reply of "Everything looks fine!" won't be helpful feedback.
- **Are subject-matter experts:** Since peer review is mainly about vetting concepts, choose a reviewer who is as well-versed in your topic as you are. They don't need to be the world's foremost authority, but they should have enough knowledge to tell you if your ideas are technically sound. Consider running your draft by multiple reviewers with differing levels of expertise: longtime practitioners may not be able to assess whether your material is accessible to less experienced folks, while people who haven't been in the industry as long won't have the historical context to know whether your takes are new, or just new to them.

You may want to ask a member of your target audience to read your draft as well, to see what's hitting and missing your intended readers. More technical or complex books may benefit from multiple perspectives from both target readers and subject-matter experts; less technical books may only need a more casual review.

What to ask

Regardless of who you ask to review your work, be clear about what you need (and don't need) from them. Ask them to:

- **Check for conceptual validity:** The best insights your peer reviewers can provide are in the realm of *making sure you sound like you know what you're talking about.* That's it! Ask them if there were any spots where they got lost or noticed incorrect or confusing information.
- **Suggest additions and deletions:** People outside your own head are great for spotting what you've missed, whether that's an industry resource, an expert to interview, a stronger example, a recommended tool or process, or simply additional context. They're also great at spotting places where you might be repeating yourself, overexplaining, or underexplaining.
- **Avoid copyediting:** Humans are spectacularly bad at ignoring typos (once they see them). Your reviewers may get distracted with making edits to punctuation and spelling, even though the scale of review you need is much, much broader. They may also make edits that don't align with your publisher's style guide, so the effort will have been wasted. Reassure your peer reviewers that you are still in the editing process, and that all typos will be addressed before publication. (Except for the ones that sneak through. But that's never happened to us. Nope. Not even once.)

On top of getting marvelous feedback from trusted colleagues, peer review is also one of your early forays into marketing: your peer reviewers are also potential endorsers. Involve them in your project early on, and they'll be rooting for your success the whole way through.

Technical editing

If your book has language or ideas that are specific to a technical discipline (such as, oh, web design and development), it's a good idea to conduct a technical edit: a round of editing that looks at (and *only* at) the technical content of the manuscript.

Technical content varies widely in web topics: your book may have lines of JavaScript or audit spreadsheets, explanations of service workers or content management systems, discussions of font families or assistive technology. The type of technical content, the level of detail or specialization, and the subject-matter expertise of your editorial team (if you have one) are all factors in the kind of technical edit your book may need.

At ABA, if a manuscript has blocks of code in it, we'll bring in a technical editor who specializes in the given language. The tech editor reviews just the code and the text that supports the code, checking for accuracy and ensuring the author hasn't made any errors or misplaced any semicolons. This can get complicated, because—did you know?—not everyone on the internet agrees on web standards, especially when common usage differs slightly from the spec. (Do not ask us what our house style is for formatting plugin names. Do not ask us whether *flexbox* should be capitalized. Do not ask us about the time we created a new style for console output. *We do not want to talk about it.*)

While we run our tech edits about halfway through the editing process, you could easily combine them with your peer review, or ask your peer reviewer to conduct technical edits, if that's their area of expertise. If you're self-publishing, or your editing team doesn't conduct technical edits, consider hiring an expert in the technical aspect of your book to give it a look. If you're writing about code, ask them to test it too. Tech editors—and peer reviewers—are there to make sure what you've written is sound, sensible, and reliable.

COLLABORATING WITH EDITORS

If you are working with a publisher, they will assign an editor or a team of editors to work with you on your book. This is very exciting, because now an expert in communication and publishing is joining forces with you, an expert in tech. Your editor probably won't be involved in your drafting phase, but once you've completed your first draft, you'll begin working in earnest with them on what is likely to be an intensive, collaborative, and sometimes challenging editorial process.

If you aren't working with a publisher (or yours doesn't have a robust editorial process), consider hiring a freelance editor—your book will truly benefit from an objective, professional eye. Where do you find a freelance editor, you might ask? Behold:

- **Check the Editors of Color database** (http://bkaprt.com/ysw40/05-03/). Not only is this site jam-packed with excellent editors, but it also allows you to filter your search based on topics and types of editing.
- **Check social media platforms.** Editors aren't shy about advertising their services. If you know at least one person in editing or publishing, you can check their connections and hashtags for other links into online publishing communities.
- **Check with your colleagues in content design and copywriting.** They may provide side-gig editing services or know folks who do. (A gentle reminder: editing is a very specific skill! Make sure you work with someone who is familiar with the editorial concepts discussed in this chapter.)
- **Check the websites of authors whose style you like.** Some authors offer book-editing services themselves. If they've self-published, they may have worked with freelance editors they can recommend.

If you aren't working with any editors at all, we strongly encourage you to adapt the processes and habits in this section for your own use. Every editorial pass—the phases of which we'll discuss in a moment—will lend another layer of polish and professionalism to the final product.

Your editor's job

A good editor is a collaborative partner. They are here to help you develop, enhance, and polish the raw ideas—and trust us, they *are* raw—that you poured into your draft. Editors bring two necessary elements to the book:

- **Writing and publishing expertise.** Editors know what readers want, what excellent writing looks like, and exactly what kind of work it takes to turn a bad first (or second, or seventeenth) draft into a great book.
- **Not being you.** Editors can approach your manuscript bright-eyed and baggage-free, the way your audience will: with neither the bone-deep knowledge of your topic nor the harrowing memories of the drafting process.

In essence, your editor will assess your content objectively, bridging the gap between what you want to communicate and what the reader needs to hear. Their mission is to help you package your intentions and ideas in a way that will best reach your audience.

To that end, when you begin working with an editor, they'll ask a lot of questions in an effort to understand your goals, your audience, and the problems you're trying to solve. If it feels like backtracking to you—after all, you did all this work back in Chapter 2—remember that having a shared vision for the book will enable both of you to make informed choices in service to that vision.

Your editor should push you. Gently. Ish. They should poke holes in your theories, demand additional explanations, question your sources, and generally tear your draft into ribbons. But, you know, *kindly*. If everything goes well, you'll be a little embarrassed that your first draft was ever shown to another human soul—and you'll be grateful for your editor's insights and psyched for future editing rounds. You and your book will be better for it, we promise.

Editing as conversation

Good editing should feel like a conversation—one based on shared goals, mutual respect, and a willingness to listen (and learn). But even with this understanding, it can be challenging to accept edits. Writing is an act of vulnerability—you're putting your ideas out there, maybe for the first time, only to find out that they aren't coming across as effectively (or as accurately) as you thought. It's rough on the ego, especially if you're not used to having your work critiqued.

Here's some advice for getting through editing rounds:

- **Genuinely listen.** Nobody loves criticism, but people who can accept criticism openly, gracefully, and thoughtfully are better writers for it. If you are expecting only positive feedback, or are only looking to an editor to confirm your own opinions, you will have neither a productive editing relationship nor a good book. Positive, constructive feedback is a valuable tool for nurturing your book.
- **Ask questions.** Whatever edits you receive, recognize that they are not commandments—you don't have to accept every suggestion wholesale. If you disagree with an edit, say so. Maybe you don't understand why the editor is asking for a particular change. Maybe they've misunderstood your intent, and the edit would alter the meaning. Maybe the edit strays too far from your voice or your goals. Explain your reasoning, ask for clarification, and see if you can find alternatives together. Bringing up your concerns can help the editor reconsider and come back with a stronger edit that's more on your wavelength.
- **Be flexible.** It's possible your editor will put their foot down about a particular change. This doesn't happen often, in our experience—we'd rather not come to tears over synonym selection—but if there's something in the manuscript that may be incorrect or harmful, a good editor won't back down. Don't be precious about your phrasings, anecdotes, or examples; trust that your editor knows how your audience may take (or mistake) your meaning.

While it's important to be open to feedback you might initially disagree with, it's also important to recognize that, well, not all editors are good. Good editors know how to deliver feedback respectfully. As editor Adaobi Obi Tulton told us, "Critiques may bruise your ego, but they should be helpful, not hurtful." If an editor hasn't worked on their own biases, or prioritizes pedantry above all else, you may find yourself dealing with rude, aggressive, or unfair feedback.

This is, unfortunately, more likely to happen if you identify as a member of a marginalized group and your editor comes from a dominant group (most editors do). Author Ijeoma Oluo underscored this in her newsletter *Behind the Book*:

> *"If you are a person of color, there is a good chance that you will have trouble finding an editor who can understand your lived experience, language, politics, or messaging to nearly as great a degree as an editor of color can…. You have to be really sure of yourself and your voice and be willing to overly communicate where you're coming from because even the best white editor just* won't get it *sometimes." (http://bkaprt.com/ ysw40/05-04/)*

If your editor doesn't respect you or your project, do not work with them. That's easier said than done for writers of color, who may not have as many choices when it comes to getting published or working with editors. But remember: you can and should trust your experience—you are *right* to push back on editors who want you to write in a voice that isn't yours.

A good editor is on your side. If you and your editor both enter into the working relationship with open hearts and open minds, the result will be a much better final product.

Editorial phases

A truly rigorous editorial process is made up of multiple phases of scrutiny, each getting progressively more granular. Think of the process as a series of filters to ensure that everything—from big-picture thinking all the way to punctuation-level details—gets its due. Reviewing your whole work, multiple times, with a different area of focus in mind each round, will help ensure a comprehensive edit.

At A Book Apart, our editorial phases are:

1. Developmental editing
2. Line editing
3. Copyediting
4. Proofreading

While other publishers may differ on the phase names or durations, this should give you an idea of what to expect no matter whom you're working with—even if it's only yourself. The logistics of each editorial phase will depend on the length and scope of your book, the strengths of your draft, and your level of detail.

Developmental editing

The developmental edit (sometimes called a conceptual edit) focuses on the bird's-eye view, ensuring that the manuscript is conceptually whole, logically written, and structurally sound. It's about creating a strong foundation for the more granular edits that will follow.

In this phase, pay attention to the book's structure, narrative flow, ideas, and clarity. Does it make sense? Is it doing the job you set out to do? Will your intended readers understand its lessons? Do the ideas build on one another as they're presented? Is there enough material, or too much? Are there areas that need more research? No matter how strong you thought your first draft was when you finished it, you'll now be forced to face your narrative gaps, logical leaps, repeated paragraphs, and incomplete ideas. You wrote a glorious hot mess; we are sorry to inform you that the developmental edit phase will see you rewriting it.

Developmental edits typically take up more time than any other editorial phase. A manuscript might spend several weeks with an editor, then several weeks with the author—and this back-and-forth might happen two or three times. Give yourself plenty of time here. Take frequent breaks to let revisions gel.

Since you're keeping your edits high-level at this phase, try to ignore fiddly things like typos, sentence construction, word choice, and punctuation. Rewriting sentences can certainly help clarify ideas and rework structure, but try not to get bogged down in polishing when you're still constructing. There's no point in correcting typos in a sentence destined for deletion.

Developmental edits are done when—forgive our imprecision here—the book *feels* conceptually solid. When you've stopped moving pieces around, when you're done repairing logical gaps, when you start spending more time on sentences rather than sections—that's when it's time for line edits.

Line editing

Where developmental edits suggest conceptual changes—like changing heading hierarchy, dividing chapters, and rearranging sections—line edits busy themselves with language. Line edits (sometimes called stylistic edits) get into the guts of your ideas. Truly, you're asking many of the same questions you asked during the developmental edit—*does this make sense, will the audience get it, is this the right way to say this*—but at the level of sentences and paragraphs, rather than sections and chapters.

In this phase, pay attention to your paragraphs and sentences. Is the language clear and inclusive? Do the sentences flow? Are the ideas connected? Are there segues between sections? Is the writing conversational and approachable? Do the examples, images, and recommendations serve the reader?

Line edits often feel a little more concrete—now you're debating *words*, not just ideas!—so these rounds tend to be very active. Marking up sentences results in more (digital) ink than the types of global changes that come up during developmental edit. Don't shy away from this! Intensive line edits are what make your book approachable, understandable, and readable.

Copyediting

By the time you hit the copyedit phase, your major revisions are done: the concepts are solid, the language is clear, and the details are accurate. The focus now is on grammar, style, and formatting.

Read your latest draft with an eye toward all those fussy details we told you to ignore earlier. Thanks to the modern marvel of word-processing software, you're unlikely to have made many spelling errors, but software still struggles to catch homophones, typos, and contraction mistakes. (How often does autocorrect wreck everything? Too ducking often.) Better get human eyeballs on it before you leave an *l* out of *public*.

As for grammar and punctuation, we must now reveal an arcane and carefully guarded secret: *it's all made up.* That's right: grammar is subjective, constantly changing, and way more permissive than you might think. That's a good reason, if you're not working with an editorial team, to adopt a specific writing style guide (see the Resources section). A style guide means someone else has already made all the fiddly decisions about how to style lists, when to write *percent* instead of *%,* and whether you should use an Oxford comma (spoiler: yes). Following a style guide means you'll style your writing consistently, everywhere in the book, without having to second-guess yourself.

You should also use the copyediting phase to fact-check. People should only publish true statements, which you'd think goes without saying, but Picard-facepalm-dot-gif. Stick to the facts, and ensure you've correctly spelled proper names (people, places, products), used people's identified pronouns, accurately captured quotations, and provided the right URLs for links.

Proofreading

Proofreading is what many non-writers first think of when they hear "editing"—the typo corrections and punctuation changes that one performs before sending an email or turning in a design artifact. But, as we've seen, editing is considerably more in-depth than that, and proofreading is but the final frontier in a fairly long journey.

Use your proofreading round to prepare your manuscript for production. Examine it with a fine-tooth comb, ensuring that there are no stray marks, missed typos, formatting errors, extra spaces, or other mistakes that could snarl up the final product.

For example, Microsoft Word loves to change curly quotation marks to prime marks for no reason at all, even if they've been correctly styled the entire editorial process thus far (*you had one job, Word*). Proofreading is the last editing round to catch that sort of thing (though the book should be proofed again once it's in layout).

Despite this final line of defense, the truth is that no book is completely free of errors when it goes into publication. We cringe to think how many times we've misspelled a name or lost an apostrophe, only to be called out on Twitter after the book is in readers' hands. If you're self-publishing, consider keeping a spreadsheet—a.k.a. an *errata log*—to track any changes you want to make, before a second printing or to digital files.

OKAY, *NOW* YOU'RE DONE

This whole "writing a book" deal may feel like it has lasted forever: as if the drafting weren't enough of a slog, we then insisted you perform multiple rounds of editing, like some kind of conscientious person with quality standards and a desire to put thoughtful work out into the cold, uncaring universe. *Rude.*

But we're sure it's all worth it. Could you have flung off your first thoughts into the void and called yourself a published author without once reading back your work? Sure. (Have you *been* on the internet? They'll let anyone type there.) But by giving yourself the gift of time, objectivity, and perspective, you've shaped your raw thoughts into something truly special. Your book has grown into the best version of itself it can be.

And while you're now at the end of your text adventure, you're not quite published yet. It's time to look at how to turn your manuscript into an actual product.

6 PREPARING FOR PUBLICATION

> *When I was still an aspiring author, I erroneously believed that I had to spend a lot of time on the details: book design, cover design, choosing fonts and tools. These are options, not mandates. The only tools a self-published author needs to publish a book is a word processor (or text editor), a person to edit or proofread their work, and a way to export their file to PDF.*
>
> *The content of your eBook matters above all else. I have purchased eBooks at USD$39 that were double spaced, and written in Arial, 14-point font. But the value I got from the content was immeasurable. I did not notice, or care, if the cover design was made from a Microsoft Word template.*
>
> —STEPHANIE MORILLO

WITH YOUR CONTENT COMPLETE—and amazing, we are certain!—you can turn your attention to the logistics of production, publishing, and distribution. This is an exciting stage: it's all about packaging up your book so it can reach your eager readers. And no matter your resources, budget, and taste, there are plenty of formatting and selling options to choose from.

The trouble with options is that you now have a trillion decisions to make, from your front matter to your font size to your paper quality to your marketplaces. On the other hand, the writing is finished, and after several chapters, that calls for some rejoicing! If you haven't celebrated that milestone, please put down this book and go do so before you continue. Then get ready to learn about the wild, wonderful world of making books.

PRODUCTION

First, let's get into what's typically involved in producing a book—that is, assembling its components, designing its interior and exterior, and laying out the text. If you're working with a publisher, they'll have requirements around how to deliver your final manuscript draft to their production team. By this point, they may not even need you to necessarily *do* anything—their editor or project lead will often handle getting the final draft over to production.

We'll give you an idea of what to expect when working with a publisher—and help you determine your own approach if you're self-publishing.

Manuscript.final.FINAL-final.docx

In addition to your edited, completed, and stunningly brilliant manuscript, there are several other written elements that are often included in a book. If you have a publisher, they may provide these sections for you, or ask you to collaborate on them; if you're self-publishing, you may want to include (or skip) them.

First, consider the elements that usually appear at the beginning, before your text, which publishers sometimes refer to as *front matter*:

- **Title:** Oh, yeah. Remember when we talked about the working title in Chapter 3? You're gonna want to firm that up now, if you haven't already. We recommend a title that accurately reflects the book's content, above all else (and after finishing the book, you'll have a better sense of its true scope than you did when you started); titles that are specific, clear, and speak to the book's benefit to the reader are also wise. Do a quick web search to make sure your dream title isn't already taken by a market competitor, and that it doesn't get lost in an SEO ocean—a title like *Web Design* won't exactly grab the top spot on a search results page, whereas a more specific title *about* web design will have a better chance of being found. It's also handy to see if your ideal title is available as a domain name and social media handles.

- **Dedication:** Some authors like to dedicate their book to one or two individuals with a brief, personal message of thanks. We've also seen authors use this space to acknowledge the peoples on whose unceded land the book was written, which we think is a wonderful move. Like an acknowledgements section, it's a space for gratitude, but usually much briefer and more personal.

- **Foreword and blurbs:** Think of the foreword and blurbs as the ultimate testimonials. A foreword appears at the beginning of the book, introducing and giving credibility to the author (that's you), saying a bit about the content, and helping readers understand why they should read the book. Blurbs will do similar work in a much shorter format— almost like a great soundbite—and typically appear on the cover or inside jacket of a book. (We'll talk about collecting forewords and blurbs in Chapter 7.)

- **Glossary:** Some books include a glossary to define jargon or niche terms. This may appear in the front or back of the book, and is more common in books aimed at students or beginners, or on topics that are highly specialized. We don't love jargon (though it is often necessary in web work), and when we use it, we prefer to define terms in context rather than in a separate section. That said, in Eva Penzey-Moog's book *Design for Safety*, we included a list of terms at the beginning because it was important for readers to understand the very deliberate language used in discussing a sensitive topic.

There's also content that's typically found at the end of the book, after your content, also known as *back matter*:

- **Resources:** We recommend listing any books, articles, slide decks, videos, or tools that informed your thinking or are foundational to your topic, as well as any that explore ideas related to your core topic. Our only warning is to be careful when listing tools and products; these items tend to disappear or shut down more frequently than, say, books.
- **Acknowledgments:** An acknowledgments page is anywhere from a few sentences to several paragraphs, and can say anything you want (the page is your oyster). Many authors use this space to thank their early readers, their editors (aw, shucks), their partners and pets, their families and friends, their managers and coworkers, and other members of the community who encouraged them to write, supported their work, or helped them think through their topic.
- **Index:** Indexes are a list of all the people, places, and things mentioned in your book. They are typically included in the very back of professional and academic texts to help readers navigate the book's concepts on a more granular level. The index is compiled after the book is laid out (see later in this chapter) so the indexer can find the right page number. It's not essential to include indexes in ebooks, since the text is often searchable (though A Book Apart does include them, as an added layer of accessibility). If you're self-publishing and want to build an index: once the pages are finalized and sequenced in layout, read through your book while highlighting proper nouns, important concepts, and any other words you think readers may need to reference later. Note the page numbers as you proceed, then arrange the terms in alphabetical order in the back of the book.
- **About-the-Author page:** Most books include a brief biography of the author (one to two paragraphs) with relevant professional and personal details, often with a headshot. This may appear on the back cover, the back jacket panel, or as a page at the end of the book.
- **Book description:** A book description may also appear on the book's back cover, inside jacket panel, or as a part of the book's web presence. It's often written as part of the marketing process, but it's the kind of additional material you'll want to compile along with all the formal *book bits*. A good

book description should summarize what the book is about while also enticing people to read (and buy) it. If you do no other marketing, the book description can serve double duty as a concise (and compelling!) way to talk about your book.

Finally, your book may have supplementary materials that aren't a part of the actual manuscript but will ultimately support the reading of the book, such as digital worksheets, downloadable templates, shared documents, or external code samples. These items may be linked in your book text or listed in your resources section, so you'll want to make sure they're up and running as you head into production. Similarly, if you're creating a website or any social media accounts for your book—well, hopefully you've gotten started already! But now's a good time to troubleshoot and roll out.

Whatever additional sections or resources you want to include with your book, work with your editor (if you have one) to ensure these pieces end up in your manuscript file the way they need to be, and that you aren't missing anything when you head into production. (No, we do not want to talk about the time we printed *Resilient Management* without a foreword. No.)

Design and layout

Once you (or your editor) have compiled all the final manuscript elements, now begins the half-art, half-science of visually presenting all that content in page format. Publishing houses have well-established processes for layout and composition, so if you're working with a publisher, you won't likely have much visibility or input into this phase. If you get to provide input on the cover (yeah, buddy), that's usually the most interaction you'll have concerning the book's design. If you're self-publishing, of course, you can handle design yourself or hire a designer.

This isn't to say you *must* design your book, especially if you don't have the time, resources, or inclination—it's just another consideration. If you *do* want to be involved with design, here are some useful questions to ponder on your own or discuss with a designer:

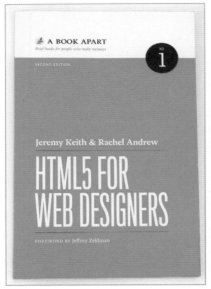

FIG 6.1: The design for A Book Apart's covers (left) took cues from Penguin's Vintage series covers (like this one for George Orwell's *1984*, right). Photograph by Sally Wilson (http://bkaprt.com/ysw40/06-03/), **CC BY-SA** 2.0 (http://bkaprt.com/ysw40/06-04/), via Wikimedia Commons.

- What format do the book's images need to be in? Are they photographs, diagrams, tables, or a mix?
- Does the book need to be produced using full color?
- What kind of design element(s) does the book need to indicate new chapters or sections (if any)?
- How will the title be displayed on the book cover?
- Do I need original art for the cover or interior sections?

When Jason Santa Maria first set out to design the look and feel for A Book Apart's books, he took a spark of inspiration from Penguin's vintage paperbacks for their aesthetic and approachability (**FIG 6.1**) (http://bkaprt.com/ysw40/06-01/). From ABA's very first title, he designed the cover so that each book would:

- have a connection to and cohesion within the larger library, regardless of how large the library grew;
- use color consistently and boldly, with thoughtful, unpretentious design elements adaptable from title to title.; and
- be portable and easy to handle; the 5.5" × 8.5" pages and comfy margins leave room for marginalia and doodles and a reading experience unobstructed by thumbs (http://bkaprt. com/ysw40/06-02/).

This little reverie about how our books came to be, design-wise, isn't (just) meant to show off our snazzy covers—it's also meant to give you an idea of what might go into thinking about your book's look. Even neat, uncomplicated design (*especially* neat, uncomplicated design) still needs consideration.

Polishing your styles

Whether you want *publishing* to mean sending your wonderful book to friends and family as a PDF or posting it as Markdown on GitHub, styling is essential. It gives logical and visual structure to your writing, making it easier for readers to understand and enjoy your content.

Publishers generally have established manuscript styling (as we saw in Chapter 5), which means they also have established styling for layout and composition. A Book Apart has more than twenty paragraph styles and twenty character styles set up in Microsoft Word to cover formatting circumstances ranging from basic (chapter titles, bolding) to esoteric (URLs linked in an epigraph, inline code in a third-level heading). Not all books use every style—most top out around a dozen—and every once in a long while, we have to create a new style to accommodate a visual distinction that is truly unique.

This extensive style management is the first step in producing books at ABA. We've mapped our manuscript styles to the InDesign templates we use to compose each book (**FIG 6.2**). This allows us to efficiently translate a Word document into a first-draft layout for printing (or for ebook formats). It's a little bit like using a stylesheet; when we apply the Chapter Title style

FIG 6.2: A Book Apart's character styles as applied in Word (left) and in InDesign (right).

to text in Word, InDesign recognizes it as a chapter title and automatically styles it correctly in layout.

No matter how many or how few styles you're working with, check to make sure:

- you're using established styles consistently,
- you've checked your heading hierarchy, and
- there aren't any duplicate styles in use.

The most essential styling considerations exist to make things clear, consistent, and as simple as possible. A manuscript without a lot of visual or hierarchical elements might only need five or six styles (title, headings, subheadings, and a few character styles). A Book Apart's book compositor, Ron Bilodeau, encourages us to consider what's *really* needed and not to go beyond that. Keeping things simple makes for a more manageable manuscript that's easier to move from editing into production.

Copyright

If you're self-publishing in the US, your work is automatically copyrighted from its creation (http://bkaprt.com/ysw40/06-05/). If you want to be able to sue for any infringements of your work, you need to register that copyright. Registering a single book with the US Copyright Office (as of this writing) costs $45 and can be done fairly quickly on their website (http://bkaprt. com/ysw40/06-06/).

Copyright notices aren't *required* by law, but they're beneficial because they indicate that a work is protected by copyright and identify the copyright owner and year of publication. Writing a copyright notice is also straightforward. A publisher will likely use standard copy they've developed, like the extremely clear and concise language we use (flip or scroll back toward the front of this book to see what we mean). Use elements from your favorite book's copyright page as a template to start from.

As we discussed in Chapter 3, if you're working with a publisher, you'll want to verify the copyright terms when signing the contract. The publisher will take it from there to obtain and process the copyright details.

ISBN

An International Standard Book Number (ISBN) is a thirteen-digit numeric code that serves as a global, unique product identifier for your book. It's used any time a publisher, library, or bookseller (or any other reseller or distributor) wants to order, list, track sales records, and manage inventory of your book.

Each ISBN is unique to an edition of a title (paperback, hardcover) or format (audiobook, ebook). For example, when A Book Apart publishes a paperback, an ebook, and an audiobook of the same title, we assign a unique ISBN to each product.

If you're working with a publisher, they will be your book's *publisher of record*, which means they are the entity in whose name the book's ISBN is registered; they will handle securing the ISBN number(s) for your book and its relevant formats and editions as necessary.

If you're self-publishing, you have a few options. You can forgo an ISBN if you're publishing your work in ebook format only or if you don't plan on selling your book. The bottom line from our perspective: you want your book to have an ISBN if you want to sell it and if you want (more) folks to find and read it.

If you're selling through a publishing service like Amazon Kindle Direct Publishing (KDP) or IngramSpark, they'll offer an ISBN as part of their service, and will appear as the publisher of record. In the US, you can get your own ISBN for roughly $125 (at the time of writing) through Bowker, the official source of ISBNs in the US and its territories (http://bkaprt.com/ysw40/06-07/). In Canada, you can go through Library and Archives Canada (http://bkaprt.com/ysw40/06-08/); otherwise, go through the International ISBN Agency (http://bkaprt.com/ysw40/06-09/).

PUBLISHING METHODS

So, what does *publishing* mean, exactly? Most succinctly (and academically), it's the process through which content is made available to the public. Traditionally, publishing referred to the distribution of printed works like books, newspapers, and magazines. With the advent of digital information systems, the scope expanded to include electronic publishing such as ebooks, micropublishing, websites, blogs, video games, etc. The commercial publishing industry ranges from hundreds of large multinational conglomerates to thousands of small independent organizations (*hi!*).

Because book-publishing methods are so wide-ranging, we're going to cover the ones we know best for both working with a publisher and going your own way. We speak to both print and ebooks, because, well, we know how to successfully create and sell both. When working with a publisher, both formats will almost always be produced. When self-publishing, you'll want to consider several variables before committing to one format over another (or both). It might seem easier or cheaper to produce only an ebook, but that's not necessarily the case and depends on many factors. We know that's not the most clear-cut advice, but it's why we're going to talk through some popular options.

Printing your book

If you're not working with a publisher, you have a few options for printing your book on your own. (Not counting starting a bespoke printing operation on the side, which would be so cool but frankly sounds like a lot of work.)

One option is to print the books yourself through small-scale, online custom printers or local print shops. The teams who run them are often some of the most helpful, insightful, and kind folks. Also, remember zines? We mean from the 1990s, but if you're not an old like we are, maybe you remember them from 2020 (http://bkaprt.com/ysw40/06-10/). We also want to reiterate what Stephanie Morillo noted at the beginning of this chapter: you can save your book as a PDF, take it to a printer, and sell the printed copies online. Heck, you don't even need to print it: you can sell the PDF as a download from your site. Both of those count as publishing your book, and you can make them happen *right now*!

Another option is to use a one-stop-shop publishing service, such as Amazon KDP, IngramSpark, BookBaby, Lulu, and Blurb (with more emerging all the time). These services allow you to create—and sell—your book in both print and digital formats (more on that soon). For printed books, you'll be able to choose from standard paperback and hardcover sizes, paper stock options, and a range of print reproduction quality—without having to meet minimum requirements for print volume. These services make it super easy for authors to produce and publish their own books—and for readers to then buy those books. We're glad such services exist because they disrupt some of the gatekeeping in publishing.

That said, large platforms like Amazon can also bind you to some extremely convoluted terms of service (like exclusivity and mediocre royalty splits)—terms that don't favor the author and that perpetuate power hoarding, elitism, and a scarcity mindset. Please read any and all terms of service carefully before you begin.

Decisions, decisions

When you're self-publishing, the choices for *what* and *how* to print can feel overwhelming. Ultimately the decisions you'll make are all about what you want (it's your book, after all!) and what you can afford (oh right, budget). A few essential print elements worth considering:

- **Design and layout.** How do you want your book to look and feel? Perhaps you want to use thematic colors or graphic elements to accentuate each chapter. You may want to hire a designer to create a customized cover or interior layout; designers who work in print may also have suggestions for how you could or should print your book.
- **Color.** Should you print in full color or grayscale? If you have lots of images and design elements, you'll presumably want them to appear in color. Most printers and print-on-demand services will offer at least both a standard and a premium option for printing in full color (and sometimes a range of options and price points in between). Grayscale is the least expensive option, and a perfectly good one, as long as what you're trying to convey visually is still clear without color.
- **Paper stock weight.** What paper thickness is ideal for your book cover and interior pages? The best advice we can give here is to choose what fits your budget. Unless you're printing a super-fancy coffee-table book, you can get away with very affordably priced paper stock. A Book Apart books use a 100# dull coated card stock for the cover (think postcard) and a 68# uncoated text stock for the interior pages.
- **Paper stock finish.** For card or cover paper stock, coating protects the paper and ink used to print the book and is typ-

ically available in glossy or dull (also called matte). For text or interior paper stock, coating may also protect the paper and ink used, but really isn't necessary, in our experience; if you remember your high school textbooks, you know the sheen of coated interior pages.

One of the best tips we can offer here is to find *your* favorite books and use them as a reference. Does your favorite paperback have a cover with French flaps and clean-cut interior page edges (like our books)? No flaps? Rough-cut page edges? You can go to a local print shop to ask for advice about print options, paper stock, color quality, and print-run pricing—information you can use, of course, to print with them or to make choices with a third-party print provider.

No matter what route you take for printing your own book, make sure to check your printer's requirements and specifications so you know exactly how to export (and deliver) your final book file.

Creating an ebook

Publishers also work with ebook producers, either in-house or by contract. And if you're self-publishing, you *can* produce your own ebook. Is it doable? Yes. Is it easy? Hell, no. Like, technically you can export an EPUB from Microsoft Word if it's a verrry plain and simple book (think: no graphics or art, and basic styling). But, if you want to create anything other than an EPUB version of your Word manuscript, you'll need a basic working knowledge of HTML or EPUB languages.

Have we lost you yet? Let's actually back up just a bit: an *ebook* is an electronic book. Okay, maybe we don't need to back up *that* much—but the term usually describes a book you can read in a digital format. The most common file formats are EPUB, MOBI, AZW/AZW3, IBA, and PDF. (There are a handful of other less common formats you might see from time to time, but not often enough to dive into here.) When we sell an ebook at A Book Apart, it's delivered in three of the five formats just mentioned: EPUB, MOBI, and PDF.

READER/PLATFORM	EPUB	MOBI	PDF
Amazon Kindle		X	X
Apple OS and iOS	X	X	X
Barnes & Noble Nook	X		X
Windows	X	X	X

FIG 6.3: Notable digital reading platforms and the ebook file formats they support.

The format-device-application matrix is a doozy to cross-reference, so we've put together a very high-level primer (**FIG 6.3**). You'll want to create at least a PDF of your book—it's usually the easiest to generate (as easy as clicking Save As in Word or Pages), and you can start sharing it right away. If you want to provide more format options for accessibility, reach folks who prefer using ereaders, or sell your book through major platforms (like Apple Books), you'll want to look into creating an EPUB or MOBI.

Self-serve ebook production

There are free, open-source, DIY ebook production tools like calibre (http://bkaprt.com/ysw40/06-11/) and Sigil (http://bkaprt.com/ysw40/06-12/), which have varying capabilities for editing and producing most ebook file formats. Using them requires some technical knowledge—along with fortitude for Googling answers to questions and solutions if you get stuck.

Professional output services

There are also professional, collaborative book-production tools you don't need technical know-how to use. Hederis (http://bkaprt.com/ysw40/06-13/), created by former A Book Apart book compositor Nellie McKesson, is for design-leaning folks who want extensive control over the production and output of their book (digital or print). Bookalope is a similar tool that offers less custom control for the author (http://bkaprt.com/ysw40/06-14/). Both tools cost money to use, ranging from $120 to $250 per book (at the time of this writing).

Creating an audiobook

We bet you're thinking, *Wow, these jokers want me to write a book* and *record an audio version?* Well, no, you can do whatever you like. And we'll be real: recording someone (or yourself) reading your book might be an undertaking you do *not* want. As an indie publishing house, we're not set up to record and engineer audio for every title we produce, so we rely on collaboration with those authors who want to pursue audiobooks. Mike Monteiro worked with part of his design studio crew who were adept in audio engineering to record himself reading *Design Is a Job*. Laura Kalbag collaborated with her brother Sam, who engineered the recording of *Accessibility for Everyone*. And Lara Hogan worked with a music and video production studio to record *Resilient Management*.

Creating an audio version of a book expands its accessibility and offers an additional method for engaging with its content. The few audiobooks in A Book Apart's catalog were all different (and successful!) experiments, so we thought we'd share what they taught us.

Recording the audiobook

Whether you work with an experienced production team, enlist a helpful friend, or go it alone, you'll need to choose someone to narrate your book. Maybe that's you! If so, spend a little time testing out your narration. Explore your timing, pace, and tone. Lara Hogan told us she anticipated that narrating her book might feel like presenting a talk, but the pacing turned out to be surprisingly different. If reading your entire book aloud and listening to the sound of your own voice indefinitely isn't in your wheelhouse, you can hire an audiobook narration service.

If your book has images, diagrams, or code, you'll also want to consider how to handle those elements in an audio format. Laura Kalbag summarized her images and code (almost like you would in alt text or a detailed caption) to give the listener a good idea of the visual content without robotically reciting HTML.

When you've finished the recording, you or your publisher will upload the edited audio files to a distribution service such as ACX (part of Amazon's Audible audiobook platform) or Findaway Voices. Each platform has specific and detailed requirements for file format and organization, so make sure you know what you'll need to deliver before you hit record.

Distributing the audiobook

Back in 2014, ABA decided to try publishing an audiobook—and the easiest way to do that at the time was through Amazon's Audible platform. To get the best revenue split for our author, we had to agree to a seven-year exclusivity term—meaning we had to distribute and sell the audiobook *only* through Amazon *for seven years*, shutting us out from literally dozens of other audiobook platforms.

For the last audiobook we released (and going forward), we opted to distribute through Findaway Voices. Their royalty split isn't quite as competitive as Audible's, but they push their catalog to over forty different audiobook sellers (like Google Play, Apple, libro.fm, Nook, Scribd, *and* Amazon, if you like), giving authors far more reach.

Lesson learned: no matter where or how you choose to distribute your audiobook, carefully read and consider the distribution platform's rights and revenue structures.

DISTRIBUTING YOUR BOOK

Now that your book is printed, digitized, and maybe recorded, you want to sell it to people, right? Even if your book is a free, altruistic gift of literature to the world, you still need to *get it* to people; i.e., you need a way or ways to distribute and deliver it to readers. If you're working with a publisher, they'll typically handle distribution; if not, it's (once again) all up to you.

Your publisher handles everything

If you're working with a publisher, they will have this completely set up and you won't even need to think about it until launch—then you'll want to know where your publisher is making your book available so you can share that info widely and boisterously.

Publishers like A Book Apart often sell books directly to readers. Most publishers also typically make their books available through big third-party retailers such as Amazon, Barnes & Noble, and Bookshop.org (a B-Corp retailer dedicated to the public good), as well as small- and medium-sized retailers like local, independently owned bookshops.

When a retailer, reseller, or library wants to order and stock a book, it's typically purchased through book distributors instead of from the publisher directly. As of this writing, Ingram Content Group is the largest book supplier to bookstores, retailers, schools, and libraries (http://bkaprt.com/ysw40/06-15/). Their name—which will look familiar—usually appears as IngramSpark, and lands at the top of the list when you search for self-publishing services. If listed with a distributor, your book will technically be available anywhere books are sold (provided a given retailer wants to stock your book).

Working with a publisher means you don't have to be responsible for *any* of this—but at least now you know what's going on behind the scenes.

You handle everything

If you're self-publishing, similar distribution methods can apply here. If you're using a self-publishing service such as IngramSpark, Lulu, or CreateSpace (part of Amazon KDP), your book can be listed in their distribution catalog for third-party retailers of all sizes to order, stock, and sell.

You might reach a vastly larger customer base by making your book available through Amazon and other big retailers, but then again, you might not. You *will* definitely split the revenue with those retailers, though, so it's worth doing a little math just to make sure it's the right channel for you.

No matter which distribution platform you choose (Amazon, IngramSpark, Apple Books, etc.), you'll need to make sure your digital and print files meet general and retailer-specific requirements. For print books, you'll likely be required to submit a PDF that adheres to each platform's specifications. (They'll usually offer a template for making sure your PDF is compliant). For digital files, tools like FlightDeck can help make this process easy and painless for a small fee (http://bkaprt.com/ysw40/06-16/).

You can also sell directly to readers through customizable online stores like Big Cartel, Gumroad, and Shopify. These ecommerce services often integrate with self-publishing services and personal websites, or you can link to their proprietary shop pages from your existing website. (Some also offer delivery methods for digital products like ebooks, but verify this before you get started.) These stores are fantastic for centralizing sellable goods, handling transactions and fees, and managing or syncing product fulfillment. All that wondrous ease comes at a financial cost, of course, but it's usually worth the headaches you'll avoid. Basically, you want a way to physically package and ship your print books, and digitally deliver your ebooks, with as little manual effort on your part as necessary.

A quick note about bulk sales: just like a publisher will look for ways to sell multiple copies of your book at once, so should you. Decide on a discounted rate for bulk quantities of your book and offer that as an enticement to larger companies, teams you've worked with, and conferences.

VOILÀ, YOUR PUBLISHED BOOK

Working with a publisher and self-publishing are quite different paths. Each has widely varying benefits and challenges along the way, but they both lead to the same thing: a published book. And understanding a bit about what goes into self-publishing can come in handy when navigating a relationship with an established publisher.

Dan Poynter (remember the self-publishing innovator from Chapter 1?) decided to write, produce, print, and sell his first book on his own because he couldn't find a publisher interested in a technical book about parachutes. But that led him to write and self-publish more than a hundred books—a few on parachuting, skydiving, and hang gliding, and *many* focused on helping others write, publish, and sell their own books. While Poynter never claimed that self-publishing was *easy*, he did enthusiastically encourage and inspire emerging authors to consider it a very viable path to successfully launching a book.

Whether a publisher is taking the lead, or you're self-publishing and you've settled on how you want to get your book into readers' hands, you're going to want to shout about it from the rooftops, *non?* Marketing, promoting, and, yes, selling your book is the final (and lasting) endeavor in this adventure—and it's where we're going next.

7 LAUNCHING YOUR BOOK

" When you create something from your heart, I hope you promote the hell out of it. Shout if from the rooftops. Share it with everyone. Let yourself be seen. And don't apologize for it.
—LISA OLIVERA (http://bkaprt.com/ysw40/07-01/)

MARKETING, MOST FUNDAMENTALLY, means finding the right way to have the right conversations with the right people (i.e., people who are interested in supporting you). Spoiler: you've been doing this from the moment we discussed lining up supporters for your writing journey back in Chapter 2. Now it's time to harvest the marketing seeds you (maybe unknowingly) planted along the way and create a meaningful plan for promoting and selling your book.

Here's the thing. You don't *have* to do any of this. You can skip marketing entirely if you want; we know a lot of folks find self-promotion challenging or uncomfortable. But you just did an awful lot of very excellent work to keep all to yourself! Now's no time to hide.

Most publishers offer less marketing support than authors would like—and, for a while, that included A Book Apart. In early 2017, we began working with marketing consultant Leslie Zaikis. We soon realized that we'd synced up with someone who not only knows book marketing intimately, but acts as a coach and a partner, helping ABA establish an overall strategy and create book marketing plans that fit each author's needs.

Now we've seen what a valuable investment it is to collaborate on marketing with our authors. We're going to share what we've learned from that approach to help you build and commit to a marketing plan that's right for you.

YOUR MARKETING GOALS

There is no such thing as one-size-fits-all marketing. That might sound like it would make everything harder, but it's a good thing, really. It means that for your marketing plan to work, it needs to fit *you*. And, you know what? You're probably already marketing without even knowing it. Now it's time to put intention into your efforts.

David Dylan Thomas—famous at A Book Apart for his ability to market the heck out of his work while simultaneously making it look utterly effortless—told us this:

> *If you think of marketing as frivolous or abstract, I've got news for you: it's actually very disciplined, even boring. It's sending emails. It's responding to comments. It's going on Twitter. Marketing is boring, that's the takeaway. It's not magic. It's bureaucratic. The level of bureaucracy depends on the goals you set up at the very beginning.*

Find your drive

Consider your goals for your book (rather than your goals for its content or your audience, which is what you've been focused on until now): What led you to write your book? What are you trying to accomplish for yourself? What role does your book play in your future work or career?

Our marketing plans start by asking authors to first consider what's driving their goals. Identifying one or two drivers helps to focus each goal's desired outcome. Most often, we find that marketing goals are driven by:

- **Relevance:** Elevating your (or your company's) profile and establishing (or solidifying) yourself as an expert. Defining (or expanding) the conversation around your name and work.
- **Resonance:** Creating significant impact in a community or industry. Reaching your intended audience in a meaningful way and improving their lives.
- **Revenue:** Making money. This is a common, but not *primary*, driver, for most authors. To be frank, it's quite difficult to make a ton of money from writing a book. If that's your sole motivation (please don't make it your sole motivation), you have a long and frustrating road ahead.

In truth, revenue is an underlying outcome for most any goal you have, from book sales to increased speaking fees to brand partnerships. But we encourage authors to focus on how relevance and resonance play a part in their marketing goals, regardless of any profits that might follow.

Identify your goals

Once you've determined what's driving you, it's time to define your specific goals—literally, write them all down in a list.

For example, if relevance matters to you—that is, increasing your profile—you might do that by:

- speaking at more conferences
- getting quoted in articles for popular publications
- being asked to mentor younger designers

If your goal is to create resonance, you might gauge your progress by:

- noticing how many practitioners apply your approaches and techniques

- hearing clients ask more informed questions
- encountering cleaner code, reduced energy use, or more resilient team members in your community

Look particularly at the active verbs in your goals—nouns like "exposure" aren't as helpful as "get quoted in a design blog." You can identify as many goals as you like—and if you wind up with a lot of goals, it'll help if you prioritize them so you can be flexible with your bandwidth as you begin your marketing activities. Answering the following questions will help you prioritize your goals:

- What excites me about exploring this goal?
- What makes me nervous or anxious about this goal?
- What kind of support do I already have (or need) to achieve this goal?
- How easy or challenging will it be to develop a marketing plan for this goal?
- How does this goal align with my vision for the book?

The more your answers point to a goal being exciting, supported, and aligned with your values, the higher you can prioritize the goal.

Establish your success metrics

Goals are great, but—just like in web projects—we can't tell if we've reached them if we don't measure our efforts. Some goals will be easy to measure, like sales figures and revenue, and some won't; it's still valuable to establish what metrics of success you want to pay attention to for all your goals.

For each of your goals, identify a baseline, then decide what success looks like (**FIG 7.1**). For example, if your goal is to sell more workshops, write down how many workshops you sell in a year, then how many workshops you hope to sell once your book is out there. You might want to include a timeline for checking progress, or different metrics for various points after launch.

GOAL	BASELINE	SUCCESS METRIC	STATUS: FIRST 3 MONTHS	STATUS: FIRST YEAR
Sell a lot of books	0 books sold	500 books sold	150 books sold	500 books sold
Increase my speaking fee	$1,000 per speaking engagement	$2,500 per speaking engagement	1 speaking gig booked at new rate	4 speaking gigs booked at new rate
Give a conference keynote	0 keynotes	3 keynotes	1 keynote invitation	2 keynote invitations, 1 keynote delivered
Book projects based on reputation as an author	Projects currently booked through peer referrals	1 new consulting project worth at least $30K, based on authoring a book	Incoming consulting leads that mention the book	1 new consulting project booked

FIG 7.1: Use a spreadsheet or your favorite data-organizing tool to identify your main goals and determine what it will look like to fulfill them. Doing this exercise will help you focus on marketing tasks and keep track of your book's success.

There are dozens of ways you can gauge success (and most of them involve capitalism). Mathematically articulating your marketing goals means you get to have some level of quantitative proof of success, which can feel really fulfilling! But what matters most is what success looks like to *you*. When Kat Vellos wrote her first book and sent it out into the world, she asked herself, "Does the book answer the questions I wanted it to answer?" and "Do I believe in it and am I proud of it?" Those answers are the truest indicators of success.

MARKETING CHANNELS

Remember all that writing practice we talked about in Chapter 2, when you started drafting articles and blog posts to share your ideas publicly? That's about to come in handy again!

There are dozens of marketing channels, but you don't have to get a handle on all of them. In fact, we've found that the best way forward is to choose where to focus based on what you know you can do well and what you actually enjoy doing. Ahh, how refreshing!

We're going to talk a bit about the channels we focus on the most at A Book Apart—which fall into the categories of content, community, and press—so you can get a sense of how they might work for you.

Content

Marketing through content—whether repackaging existing content or creating something new—can encompass *a lot*. Consider newsletters, blog posts, articles, interviews (both written and audio), talks, and workshops. If you've been cultivating a writing practice that includes any or all of these, you'll get even more mileage out of that practice now. Let's look at some ways you might harness existing content or develop something fresh to market your book.

Newsletters

If you already write and send out a newsletter to communicate information about your work, let people know about your next talk, speak your mind, or, say, mention the book you're writing—huzzah! Time to kick it into high gear. This is a great time to ask new people to subscribe to your newsletter or email list so they can get to know you and your book!

You can use your newsletter to:

- update readers on your writing process and progress
- share sneak peeks of your book content

- promote your launch date and encourage pre-orders (if your publisher offers that)
- collaborate or cross-promote with newsletter authors who have adjacent audiences

And there are many tech newsletters and book-recommendation newsletters out there—make sure you're subscribed to them, and (when appropriate) consider asking them if they'll promote your new book.

Blog posts and articles

If you already have a blog, fantastic—use it to talk about your book! If you've been using a blog to develop your writing practice, you'll have a foundation for crafting content to promote and support your book. You can also post complementary content from your book, such as practice exercises and templates. A set of prompts in the body of your manuscript could be turned into a worksheet you could offer on your website or in workshops (FIG 7.2).

If you've written articles in the past (or regularly write for one or more outlets), now's the time to take advantage of the relationships you've built with those publishers. You might propose writing an article that talks about supporting or complementary content to what's in your book—a win-win for both you and the publisher—or offer to do a Q&A or interview about your book.

If you're new to writing articles and want to give it a go, the process will be similar to putting a book pitch together in that you'll need to propose the article concept to a publisher and work through an editorial process. Don't fret—this is something you can do! After all, you've just written a whole book.

Talks and workshops

Hey! Did you turn a talk or workshop into your book? No? Great, then you can now take your book and turn it into a talk or workshop! You may have chapters or sections that lend themselves well to a conference or corporate event, or

FIG 7.2: In *Resilient Management,* Lara Hogan included a set of questions to ask during a manager's first one-on-one (left), which she turned into a free, downloadable resource on her consulting website (right).

new, related ideas that emerged after the editing process was complete. Take that show on the road, virtually or literally (depending on whether you're reading this in the middle of a pandemic or not). And including book copies as part of a workshop offering or speaking fee is a great way to sell more books.

During your editing process, chances are that anywhere from *some* to *a lot* of your book content was edited out for various reasons (relevance, scope, polishing, etc.)—and there might be a way to breathe a second life into that content. Just because it didn't fit in the book doesn't mean it wasn't good, relevant content—it may just need a new format. Several A Book Apart authors have incorporated cutting-room-floor content into post-launch workshops, presentations, and blog posts.

Community

Sharing your book with the communities you're already a part of hopefully won't feel like *work*, even if it does still take a bit of effort. Let's look at some ways you can lean on your communities and support crews to shine a light on your book.

Interviews

If you're an introvert like we both are, interviews might not feel like the most appealing marketing channel. But hear us out! Katel was once invited to be interviewed on a podcast about her publishing work—only to be asked questions she was excited by *and knew all the answers to*. And yet, she was nervous, because being the focus of attention isn't where she feels most comfortable. But she did it anyway, had fun with it (really!), and even got to talk about *this* book long before its launch date.

Answering interview questions means talking out loud about yourself and your experiences. It means people will hear what you have to say and, sure, they may judge you—but (way more likely) they will also relate to you, connect with your experience, and be inspired by you.

If you snag yourself an interview, it'll very likely be on a podcast, because, yes, everyone has a podcast now—from big-name brands to smaller topic-themed and industry-niche shows. Take a quick inventory of your favorite shows that typically host guests and include them in your outreach. Getting a guest spot on a podcast (or as an interviewee for a printed Q&A) is a fantastic way to talk about your book in a natural, conversational way (think: you get to show up and be yourself).

Oh, wait, did you say *you* had your own podcast? You sneaky devil! We envy your commitment to content creation. Obviously, if you have a podcast, you have a tool for self-promotion right at your fingertips—but beyond talking up your work, you can also extend that work, the way Corey Vilhauer and Deane Barker did when they turned their book, *The Web Project Guide*, into a podcast by interviewing experts on each of their chapter topics. An approach like that can widen the discourse around your subject matter without repeating the book itself. And, of course, it requires no additional work—you know, aside from running an entire podcast.

Social media

Consider all the virtual audiences you've built up over time, and where you *enjoy* spending time virtually. If you're comfortable on Twitter, tweet about your book. If you're more active on Instagram than Twitter, focus there. Oh, and don't overlook LinkedIn. It's, apparently, happening, as A Book Apart authors Erika Hall (http://bkaprt.com/ysw40/07-02/) and Preston So (http://bkaprt.com/ysw40/07-03/) can attest.

You should use your personal social media accounts to promote your book. If you want to create a new account specifically for your book, go for it—but it's not necessary, especially if your personal account already has a healthy following. You may want to spend some time gathering related content, determining the best formats for your chosen platform, or selecting pull quotes or other elements from your book to share.

Spend time on social media talking about your book in a way—and at a pace—that feels good to you. But *do talk about your book*. You can talk about the process of writing it, or discuss its topics in greater (or lesser, depending on the platform) detail, or even use social media to do book giveaways. Social posts work best when they give the reader something to do, so consider how cross-platform promotion can tie everything together. Jump into the socials anytime you can tell people to buy your book, of course, but also when they can pre-order it, subscribe to your newsletter, listen to a podcast you're on, or read a new blog post.

Events and book clubs

With mainstream publishers, post-launch events traditionally include book tours, readings, and signings. If you're marketing your own book (this is the norm), you can still schedule readings and even book club events virtually and in-person. Take an inventory of your favorite local bookstores and book clubs, and ask them if they'll host you for a reading. Reach out to any local meetups or local tech companies you may have ties to, and see if they're looking for an informal Q&A. If you live in a larger city, there may also be free community events or unconferences that would be happy to host a chat with you about your book.

Press

Press can range from the mainstream and highly visible media—such as bestseller-list sources, national magazines, big industry trade publications, and national radio and television—to smaller and more niche options, such as local, community, and industry-specific media outlets.

Pursuing press coverage can yield a big return on investment because it can create more momentum and visibility for an author and their work. Unfortunately, there's no trick here—it's a challenging channel. Only a few things really work, and their success rate is, admittedly, pretty damn low:

- Pure luck. (That's not advice. That's just how it is.)
- Spam every press outlet you can possibly think of and hope that someone responds. (We don't love this, especially as an outlet sometimes on the receiving end of this practice. That doesn't mean it won't, in rare cases, actually work. But that usually comes back to luck again.)
- If you know someone who works at a press outlet, now is absolutely the time to call in a favor or craft a personal inquiry. (Of course, knowing someone is often a mix of coincidental relationship building and, again, luck. Weird how that keeps showing up.)
- Identify writers at outlets who have written about books similar to yours and reach out to them with a specific ask. You can even pitch your own ideas (like doing an interview or author Q&A, or sharing complementary content).

That last approach is especially valuable in making progress with smaller-scale and specialized outlets where you can make a big impact. Focusing on more relevant outlets that are likely more important to your intended readers can get you a lot of (meaningful) visibility. With press, it's all about setting expectations and understanding where your effort is most impactful.

REACHING OUT

We've offered some brief suggestions to start building your communications ecosystem as you write and develop your book. Perhaps you've considered and already started creating a newsletter, and you've at least started telling people you're writing—or have written—a book, right? *Right?*

Look, if you do literally nothing else to market your book, do this one thing: activate your personal network and tell everyone you know. No, really, we mean *everyone*. And while you're telling everyone about the amazing thing you did, why not ask for a little support?

Will you endorse me?

Asking someone to write a foreword or blurb (as we mentioned in Chapter 5) for your book is a wonderful way to get people talking about, and serve as the ultimate endorsement for, your book. You'll want to ask a foreword writer to complete their endorsement before your book is designed and assembled—the foreword will need to be included along with the other front matter during book production. Blurbs can be requested and written as part of the marketing tasks (**FIG 7.3**).

Asking someone to endorse you is an honor (for most folks). It means you respect their voice in the industry and believe your readers respect them too. It will feel enticing to choose the most well-known (dare we say, famous) or well-networked contact within your reach, and it's equally appealing to choose friends you know you can count on—folks who will say yes and deliver.

Ideally, you'll identify a few people with an enchanted combination of expertise plus notoriety plus approachability plus availability. We like to encourage authors to draft a list of everyone they'd be sincerely honored and humbled to have endorse their book—everyone from your peers to dream-level celebrities. From there, identify who you can connect with (directly or via networking support), and select three to four folks to reach out to first.

> This book could truly be titled *Better Products*. Krystal Higgins beautifully debunks the myth of one-and-done onboarding approaches, and provides a practical guide to making products that welcome users over and over again.
>
> —KATE RUTTER
> Principal at Intelleto and cohost of
> What is Wrong with UX podcast

FIG 7.3: A blurb by Kate Rutter, displayed on the inside of the *Better Onboarding* book cover, and in a graphic shareable on Instagram.

Make sure your request is clear and provides details like the deadline for writing the endorsement and its necessary length (A Book Apart blurbs are twenty-five to fifty words, while forewords are roughly three hundred). Don't forget to include a copy of your book (they shouldn't endorse without having read it!)—a PDF is fine, especially since you usually need to line up endorsements before the manuscript goes to press.

Endorsements may not be very long, but remember: you're still asking for someone to spend their energy on something for free (and reading a book takes time), so you may get a "no." Rejection here is often due to timing and bandwidth; try not to take it personally, and respect the decision your potential endorser makes. When it does work out, be sure to thank the folks who contributed for their work (a great place to do that is in an acknowledgments section).

Get ready to shout from the rooftops

The best way to tell everyone you wrote a book is through a *Big Mouth List*. That's right. Your Big Mouth List is a big list of allll the folks you know, many of whom will be utterly delighted to know you are finally writing that book you always said you'd write—and they'll be honored to help spread the word. With their mouths. And through their social media accounts, probably.

Establishing this kind of list more formally will help you focus your communications and sort out what you want to say about your book (and when). The first step to creating your Big Mouth List is to quite literally list all the people you know in a spreadsheet, along with their contact information.

Consider all the contacts you have in your phone, your email address book, LinkedIn, and other social media communities. Also think about anyone and everyone you've intentionally connected with around the writing of your book, such as research sources, editors, industry experts, advice and insight providers, your supporters, your work colleagues, and other collaborators. (Note: This isn't a free-for-all to message everyone with publicly available contact information—you should have a real connection to the folks on your list.)

Once you've gathered your complete Big Mouth List, you'll want to organize it into categories to help you manage communication styles and frequency. It might look something like this:

- **Level 1:** These are the folks who you can depend on without a doubt. They'll share your book through their social media feeds and with their own contacts. This list might include anywhere from twelve to twenty people.
- **Level 2:** These are folks you know and want to keep updated. This group likely includes people you interviewed for the book, past professional contacts, non-immediate family members, and acquaintances you've interacted with more than once. This list might include anywhere from fifty to two hundred people.
- **Level 3:** This list includes everyone you've ever met (and have consent to contact). This list might include hundreds of people!

Your Big Mouth List will become invaluable, and you'll be so glad you took a bit of time to create it—especially as you get closer and closer to launch.

LAUNCH AND BEYOND

The month or so leading up to your book launch will be, from a marketing perspective, your busiest. Luckily, since you'll be done with the writing and editing by then, you can focus on building buzz by writing newsletters, coordinating blurbs, designing pull-quote graphics, and whatever other marketing efforts you've chosen.

At A Book Apart, we use a thirty-day marketing countdown checklist to help juggle the many balls that are, seemingly suddenly, in the air. You can start earlier than a month out—we hope you do! The checklist just happens to come in very handy for organizing essential outgoing marketing messages and alleviating the last-minute scramble (http://bkaprt.com/ysw40/07-04/).

Whether you use our checklist or opt for something else, we recommend tracking your to-dos and due dates. Launch day will be here before you know it!

Launch day

While we hope you've appreciated the many milestones of book-writing along the way, your book launch is the main event. The day your book is officially, formally, for-real, no-takesies-backsies out in the world is a big day—the pinnacle of everything you've been working toward. Give yourself some time to experience and enjoy what launch day means.

You should expect to do a few things on the big day:

- **Make sure readers can buy your book.** Whether you're selling through a distribution platform, directly on your website, or through a publisher, make sure you've got a link to the book to share via email and on social media. That's literally the entire point. Make sure your website is updated and functional, and that your social accounts (and email signature) call out and link to your book.

- **Get loud.** Launch day is the day when all your marketing prep comes to fruition, so send those newsletters, emails, and tweets. Thank folks like you're making an acceptance speech. Today you're free to truly whoop and holler and wave your hands around because you wrote and launched a book into the world. Go on, do it! Today's also the day you'll thank your past self for scheduling a few social media posts in advance—it's really nice not to have to worry about that stuff while you're celebrating!
- **Troubleshoot (if needed).** If you're self-publishing, you might ask a friend to help you monitor sales and any potential problems folks may run into when buying your book. It doesn't often happen, but, you know, technology. If your publisher is managing distribution and sales, make sure you're in communication with them so you can help report any issues you hear through social media or word of mouth.

Despite the milestone, we often hear from authors that launch day feels shockingly *quiet*. Aside from some wonderful words of congratulations, you probably won't hear a ton of noise that day—because no one's read the book yet! It'll take a few weeks before you hear from your soon-to-be-adoring public. Which means you can turn your attention to more celebratory matters.

Celebrate Good Times (Come On)

How long have you worked toward this book launch? How many hours did you pour into writing, editing, marketing, organizing your spice rack, and feeling general existential angst throughout this experience? You don't want to forget this moment—so find some ways to indelibly mark the occasion.

We really, really encourage you to make book cake a part of your celebration if you can (**FIG 7.4**). An honored tradition for A Book Apart authors (and authors at many publishers), it's exactly what it sounds like: a cake that looks like your book. It's so good. *It's so good.*

FIG 7.4: An array of book cakes that ABA authors commissioned for their respective launch celebrations. Starting at left, top row: *Conversational Design, Presenting Design Work, Voice Content and Usability* (ice cream, *ahem*). Middle row: *Design for Cognitive Bias* (plus a birthday!), *Cultivating Content Design* (clearly this called for meme frosting), *Expressive Design Systems* (why not add sparklers?). Bottom row: *Better Onboarding, Everyday Information Architecture, Design Is a Job.*

When Erika Hall published her second book, *Conversational Design*, she threw a big ol' party with a 1970s theme—complete with conversation pit—and, of course, a book cake. For the launch of *On Web Typography*, Jason Santa Maria invited everyone (literally) to a hip happy hour in downtown NYC. And Preston So held a virtual launch party for *Voice Content and Usability*, complete with a sneak-peek reading of his book, a lively Q&A, and an *ice cream* book cake. (Advantage of an ice cream cake: leftovers for*ever*.)

We even heard from a couple of our favorite non-ABA authors about how they made launch day special. Keah Brown spent a quiet evening with close friends, enjoying cheesecake and champagne to toast the launch of her first book and essay collection, *The Pretty One*. And Nicole Chung gathered with family, friends, and colleagues to celebrate the launch of her debut memoir, *All You Can Ever Know*—complete with, you guessed it, a book cake. See, it's a thing!

There are so many great ways to mark the momentous occasion that is officially launching a book into the world. Whether you keep it small and simple or go all out, the point is the same: take time to acknowledge, appreciate, and *celebrate* your book launch. *This is it!* And you deserve to be fussed over—even if it's you who's doing the fussing.

Document your success

Collect and save all the amazing things people say—the enthusiastic tweets, the replies to your newsletter, the comments on LinkedIn, the links to glowing reviews. Start and update a Google Doc, Dropbox folder, or similar, and drop in the love as it arrives—we call this a "kudos" document.

This might sound a little strange at first (saving...tweets?), but you'll be glad you did it. (If you're uncomfortable acknowledging praise, ask a friend to help you with the collection process.) First, it's important to recognize the results of all your hard work—documenting the positive feedback will really drive home what you've done. Second, you'll be able to turn some of the comments into testimonials and endorsements for your book. And third, it'll give you an automatic source of cheer whenever you're having a future down day. Need a boost? Read your kudos. Remember how wonderful it was to put your book out into the world!

Keep calm and market on

Now all that's left is to continue marketing your book until the heat death of the universe, or until you write another one and start this whole thing all over again, whichever comes first.

Would you like to talk about your book on an ongoing basis? Oh, good, because now it's less a marketing tactic and more a way of life. Whatever you do professionally from here on out—conduct workshops, change jobs, speak at conferences, start a company—your book will be a part of that. So there's no letting it languish: read tweets, write blog posts, keep up your newsletter, host a book club. Stay in touch with your publisher. Set an ongoing, reasonable, and realistic marketing schedule for yourself—because marketing is never *done*. We're sorry.

YOU'RE AN AUTHOR NOW

Kat Vellos believes that your book has two lives: "one with you," as you craft it, nurture it, and bring it to life, and "one with the world," as it moves beyond your loving arms and into view of eager readers. Trust in the work you've put in to make this book happen and stand in the confidence that your book will fulfill its purpose. Now you get to let go and be an author!

Because you are now, and you always will be.

We called it.

CONCLUSION

" Writing a book is power. It's a power that most people don't think they're capable of reaching, and the system doesn't make it easy to reach. But it's more possible than they think it is. If you are someone who's not used to being in a position of power, this is one way to move the needle a bit. It's not easy, but it's easier than you think.

—DAVID DYLAN THOMAS

WHEN WE SAT DOWN to draft this final section, we hemmed and hawed. We weren't sure what we wanted to say, and we were overwhelmed by the pressure of *writing the ending*. Endings, like beginnings, carry a lot of weight. And endings—when it comes to writing and publishing a book—mean sharing. Putting the work out into the world. Being vulnerable. Taking up space.

Publishing has long been about controlling who gets to write, what gets written, and how the writing is shared—in other words, who and what gets to take up space. And while today it's easier than ever to write and publish a book, there's still a long way to go to level the playing field and right past wrongs. Does this little book disrupt the chain of power? No. Does it take a tiny, transparent step in the right direction, making authorship more accessible for *everyone* who wants it? We truly hope so.

There's power in writing a book, however it comes into being, whatever shape it takes, and whoever's shelf it winds up on. If that's your goal, we hope we've shown you that it's within your reach. That there are many different, even unexpected, ways to get there. That the journey will be challenging, exciting, humbling, and rewarding. And that it's not a journey you have to take alone.

If you've got an idea, a little support, and the commitment to see the process through, you can write a book. You *should* write a book. Because your voice matters. And because the only way we can change the story of publishing—for ourselves, and for the authors who will follow us—is to write ourselves into it.

ACKNOWLEDGMENTS

WE ACKNOWLEDGE THE LAND on which this book was written: the traditional and unceded land of the Lenni-Lenape, Pawtucket, and Massa-adchu-es-et peoples.

Thank you to our stellar editors Adaobi Obi Tulton, Susan Bond, Caren Litherland, and Kumari Pacheco: you made this book absolutely soar. And to Sally Kerrigan: your developmental input and guidance is inimitable—thank you for truly coaching us toward a better book with kindness, integrity, and care.

This wouldn't have come into being without having worked with all the amazing ABA authors. Thank you for trusting us to help bring your books to life. And to the ABA authors of the future: we can't wait to work with you.

Our immense gratitude to everyone who took the time to share resources, talk to us, read our excruciating drafts, and provide their ever-brilliant feedback, including Nellie McKesson, Nicole Chung, Keah Brown, Stephanie Morillo, Malaika Carpenter, Samantha Soma, Michael Powers, Shara Rosenbalm, Corey Vilhauer, and Senongo Akpem.

We are deeply indebted to and honored by our endorsers: thanks to Adora Nwodo for her beautiful foreword; and to Karen McGrane, Tim Carmody, David Dylan Thomas, and Kat Vellos for their kind and heartfelt blurbs.

Katel would like to thank:

My sister, Melani, and mom, Jutta. Your love and support are unparalleled and unmatched. Thank you for always having my back and for inspiring me to do big things.

The brightest star in my solar system, Jon Long. I'm so grateful to share this life with you. Thank you for letting me get away with making truly the most terrible puns. And our weird little Hugo, you look like an old man in a small-dog bod.

LMM would like to thank:

Mat, for facing god and walking backward into hell with me. Ruby and Zero, for being orange and extremely good and not in trouble. My family, ever and always, for loving me even when I'm sad that I'm flying; and my mother in particular, for every single trip to the library we ever took.

RESOURCES

MYRIAD GUIDES, TOOLS, COMMUNITIES, and fonts of inspiration exist in the world of writing and publishing. We rely on and delight in the following, and we hope you will, too.

Publishing's past and present

There are many tomes dedicated to the documentation and retelling of publishing's history. An important thing we've learned in our own research is to interrogate the diversity of source and context. Here are a few that have inspired and surprised us:

- "Printing Press and Its 'Impact' on Literacy," from the University of British Columbia's community blog (http://bkaprt.com/ysw40/08-01/)
- "So, Gutenberg Didn't Actually Invent Printing as We Know It" by M. Sophia Newman (http://bkaprt.com/ysw40/08-02/)
- *The Printing Press as an Agent of Change* by Elizabeth L. Eisenstein (http://bkaprt.com/ysw40/08-03/)
- *Rebel Publisher: Grove Press and the Revolution of the Word* by Loren Glass (http://bkaprt.com/ysw40/08-04/)
- Literary Hub's ongoing commentary and critique on diversity in publishing (http://bkaprt.com/ysw40/08-05/)

Writing and creativity

Looking for inspiration? Want feedback on your ideas? Need prompts, advice, or guidance for your wordsmithing? There's plenty more where this came from:

- "Writing is Thinking" by Sally Kerrigan: From a long-time A Book Apart editor, this is one of our favorite articles about how to write (http://bkaprt.com/ysw40/02-01/).
- *The Artist's Way* by Julia Cameron: A book (http://bkaprt.com/ysw40/02-05/) and guided twelve-week course (http://bkaprt.com/ysw40/08-06/) for discovering and recovering creativity.

- *Our Endless and Proper Work* by Ron Hogan: An inspiration and philosophical look at the question, "Why do we write?" (http://bkaprt.com/ysw40/08-07/).
- *I Have Notes* by Nicole Chung: A newsletter discussing the craft of writing and advice on creative work (http://bkaprt.com/ysw40/08-08/, subscription required).
- The SLAPcollective: Writing, photography, and other art-inspired workshops for creatives of all skills and backgrounds (http://bkaprt.com/ysw40/08-09/).
- Writing prompts:
    - Magical Realism Bot, a Twitter-based story premise generator (http://bkaprt.com/ysw40/08-10/)
    - "22 Writing Prompts from The Moth" (http://bkaprt.com/ysw40/08-11/)
    - "Where Should We Begin," a game of stories by Esther Perel (http://bkaprt.com/ysw40/08-12/)
- The #Amwriting community: A hashtag used on Twitter and most other social platforms to connect to and learn from other writers, "discussing research, conferences, word counts, submissions, and publishing options...Lurking is not only allowed, but encouraged" (http://bkaprt.com/ysw40/08-13/).
- The OpEd Project: Workshops from "a community of thought leaders, journalists, commentary writers and activists who proactively share our skills, knowledge and connections across color, creed, class, age, ability, gender, orientation, and beyond [to] elevate the ideas and knowledge of underrepresented expert voices" (http://bkaprt.com/ysw40/08-14/).

Book clubs and reading groups

Virtual book clubs abound these days, and are a great way to read more, read critically, and make connections with readers and other authors. Here are a few suggestions:

- The Quarterly Group Read (http://bkaprt.com/ysw40/08-15/)
- LitHub's Virtual Book Channel (http://bkaprt.com/ysw40/08-16/)

- Rebel Book Club (http://bkaprt.com/ysw40/08-17/)
- Silent Book Club (http://bkaprt.com/ysw40/08-18/)
- New York Public Library's Virtual Book Club (http://bkaprt.com/ysw40/08-19/)
- Goodreads Choice Awards Book Club (http://bkaprt.com/ysw40/08-20/)

Editing and style guides

Whether you're editing yourself, seeking an editing partner, or just want more insight into editing practices, start here:

- Conscious Style Guide: Founder Karen Yin helps writers and editors think critically about using language—including words, portrayals, framing, and representation—to empower instead of limit (http://bkaprt.com/ysw40/08-21/).
- The Editors of Color Database: From the Conscious Style Guide, this searchable database is the ultimate resource for finding your next editor (http://bkaprt.com/ysw40/08-22/).
- Chicago Manual of Style: The standard American English writing style guide, used by many organizations (including A Book Apart) as the basis of their house style (http://bkaprt.com/ysw40/08-23/).
- Radical Copyeditor: Spiritual activist, educator, organizer, and radical copyeditor Alex Kapitan offers copyediting guidance to reinforce access, inclusion, and liberation (http://bkaprt.com/ysw40/08-24/).
- "General Principles for Reducing Bias": The American Psychological Association's guidelines for writing about all people and their personal characteristics without bias (http://bkaprt.com/ysw40/08-25/).
- The Trans Language Primer: An intersectional and community-supported guide to using language inclusive of gender, attraction, and acceptance (http://bkaprt.com/ysw40/08-26/).
- The University of British Columbia's "Indigenous Peoples: Language Guidelines": Terminology, acknowledgment, and recognition guidelines for writing about Indigenous peoples (http://bkaprt.com/ysw40/08-27/, PDF).

Publishing and promoting

Everything from high-level overviews to granular questions about every step of the publishing process:

- Popular self-publishing services:
    - IngramSpark (http://bkaprt.com/ysw40/08-28/)
    - Lulu (http://bkaprt.com/ysw40/08-29/)
    - BookBaby (http://bkaprt.com/ysw40/08-30/)
    - Amazon (http://bkaprt.com/ysw40/08-31/)
    - Hederis (http://bkaprt.com/ysw40/06-13/)
- "Designer to Author" workshop from Kat Vellos: The perfect workshop for making your nonfiction book dreams a reality (http://bkaprt.com/ysw40/08-32/).
- *Behind the Book* by Ijeoma Oluo: A newsletter shedding light on the trials and tribulations of writing a book (http://bkaprt.com/ysw40/08-33/).
- *One More Question* by Britany Robinson: A newsletter for freelance writers where she answers emails and offers pitch reviews to subscribers (http://bkaprt.com/ysw40/08-34/).
- "How to Get Your Book into Public Libraries and Why it Matters," from the Author Learning Center: A brief guide for ensuring your book is available through public libraries—especially handy for self-publishers (http://bkaprt.com/ysw40/08-35/).
- *The Developer's Guide to Book Publishing* by Stephanie Morillo: Insights into the tech publishing landscape and thoughtful guidance for developers (and others!) aspiring to publish their writing.

- *The Self-Publishing Manual: How to Write, Print and Sell Your Own Book* by Dan Poynter: Though the methodologies have changed since its debut in 1979, this manual provides no-nonsense advice for how to self-publish in any genre.
- *So You Want to Publish a Book?* by Anne Trubek: A crisp view of the publishing industry and how to navigate it as a first-time author, from query letter to launch.
- *Before and After the Book Deal: A Writer's Guide to Finishing, Publishing, Promoting, and Surviving Your First Book* by Courtney Maum: A comprehensive reference to the nuts and bolts of getting your first book published, with input from more than 150 contributors.
- Sidebar Saturday: A blog "where the practice of law meets the profession of writing," to help you better understand publishing law (http://bkaprt.com/ysw40/08-36/).
- A Book Apart's 30-Day Marketing Countdown: Developed in partnership with marketing consultant Leslie Zaikis, this checklist of marketing tasks will keep you on track in the lead-up to your launch day (http://bkaprt.com/ysw40/08-37/)

REFERENCES

Shortened URLs are numbered sequentially; the related long URLs are listed below for reference.

Chapter 1

01-01 https://en.wikipedia.org/wiki/History_of_writing

01-02 https://ancientegyptonline.co.uk/scribe/

01-03 http://en.chinaculture.org/library/2008-02/06/content_46431.htm

01-04 https://en.wikipedia.org/wiki/History_of_printing

01-05 https://www.indiebound.org/book/9781568601359

01-06 https://www.publishersweekly.com/pw/by-topic/industry-news/Obituary/article/68581-obituary-dan-poynter.html

01-07 https://selfpublishingadvice.org/history-of-self-publishing/

01-08 https://www.nytimes.com/interactive/2020/12/11/opinion/culture/diversity-publishing-industry.html

01-09 https://blog.leeandlow.com/2020/01/28/2019diversitybaselinesurvey/

01-10 https://www.seattletimes.com/entertainment/post-hill-press-goes-on-with-book-by-officer-in-taylor-raid/

01-11 https://www.clmp.org/publishers-that-champion-writing-by-people-of-color/

01-12 https://www.whitesupremacyculture.info/one-right-way.html

Chapter 2

02-01 https://alistapart.com/article/writing-is-thinking/

02-02 https://abookapart.com/blogs/press/get-to-know-krystal-higgins

02-03 https://www.patreon.com/posts/47373905

02-04 https://www.danroam.com/my-books

02-05 https://www.theartistswaybook.com

02-06 https://twitter.com/JennMJacksonPhD/status/1446845539245510665

02-07 https://www.masterclass.com/articles/how-to-find-a-writing-group#6-tips-for-finding-a-writing-group

Chapter 3

03-01 https://order.webproject.guide/

03-02 https://www.stephaniemorillo.co/product-page/the-developer-s-guide-to-book-publishing

03-03 https://docs.google.com/forms/d/e/1FAIpQLSez_GOkjzXchGsWqv3noES-vdSgZn28vTtxj78vzhTYqfaUEoA/viewform

03-04 https://www.strongfeelings.co/episodes/on-a-journey-to-happiness-with-keah

Chapter 4

04-01 https://twitter.com/beep/status/601352909989801984

04-02 https://www.researchgate.net/publication/200772468_Identifying_the_organization_of_writing_processes

04-03 https://twitter.com/carlam_jimenez/status/1394701599134543873?s=20

04-04 https://ijeomaoluo.substack.com/p/theres-never-a-good-time-to-write

04-05 https://msw.usc.edu/mswusc-blog/diversity-workshop-guide-to-discussing-identity-power-and-privilege/

Chapter 5

05-01 https://www.mcsweeneys.net/articles/an-interactive-guide-to-ambiguous-grammar

05-02 https://accessibility.perpendicularangel.com/ux-writer/image-alt-text-and-svg-titles/

05-03 https://editorsofcolor.com/database/

05-04 https://ijeomaoluo.substack.com/p/part-2-whats-it-like-to-write-a-book

Chapter 6

06-01 http://bookpretty.blogspot.com/2014/07/the-penguin-books-color-code.html

06-02 https://v4.jasonsantamaria.com/articles/announcing-a-book-apart/

06-03 https://commons.wikimedia.org/wiki/File:Nineteen_Eighty-Four_cover_by_Penguin.jpg

06-04 https://www.wikidata.org/wiki/Q19068220

06-05 https://copyright.gov/help/faq/faq-general.html#automatic

06-06 https://www.copyright.gov/registration/

06-07 https://www.myidentifiers.com/

06-08   https://www.bac-lac.gc.ca/eng/services/isbn-canada/Pages/create-account-isbn-canada.aspx

06-09   https://www.isbn-international.org/

06-10   https://www.salon.com/2020/08/10/zines-fan-magazine-comeback/

06-11   https://calibre-ebook.com/

06-12   https://sigil-ebook.com/

06-13   https://www.hederis.com/

06-14   https://bookalope.net/index.html

06-15   https://nonfictionauthorsassociation.com/list-of-book-distributors-and-wholesalers/

06-16   https://ebookflightdeck.com/

Chapter 7

07-01   https://www.instagram.com/p/CUtbQBml776/

07-02   https://www.linkedin.com/posts/erikahall_just-enough-research-2e-activity-6849379532005367808--bjR

07-03   https://www.linkedin.com/posts/prestonso_voicecontent-activity-6835975644854173696-tYaX/

07-04   https://docs.google.com/document/d/1GXJ3ixY9Vz5S9oiMXJqzQkoa-QOiptvLiZAuJyk_HtDo/

Resources

08-01   https://blogs.ubc.ca/etec540sept10/2010/10/30/printing-press-and-its-impact-on-literacy/

08-02   https://lithub.com/so-gutenberg-didnt-actually-invent-the-printing-press/

08-03   https://www.indiebound.org/book/9780521299558

08-04   https://www.indiebound.org/book/9781609808228

08-05   https://lithub.com/tag/diversity/

08-06   https://juliacameronlive.com/the-artists-way/

08-07   https://beltpublishing.com/products/our-endless-and-proper-work-starting-and-sticking-to-your-writing-practice

08-08   https://newsletters.theatlantic.com/i-have-notes/

08-09   https://www.theslapcollective.org/workshops

08-10   https://twitter.com/magicrealismbot

08-11 https://www.humorthatworks.com/how-to/22-writing-prompts-from-the-moth/

08-12 https://www.estherperel.com/where-should-we-begin-the-game

08-13 http://www.johannaharness.com/p/blog-page.html

08-14 https://www.theopedproject.org/

08-15 https://insiders.bookriot.com/the-quarterly-group-read/

08-16 https://lithub.com/author/thevirtualbookchannel/

08-17 https://rebelbook.club/about/

08-18 https://silentbook.club/blogs/blog/virtual-silent-book-club

08-19 https://www.nypl.org/virtualbookclub

08-20 https://www.goodreads.com/group/show/87303-goodreads-choice-awards-book-club

08-21 https://consciousstyleguide.com/

08-22 https://editorsofcolor.com

08-23 https://www.chicagomanualofstyle.org/home.html

08-24 https://radicalcopyeditor.com/

08-25 https://apastyle.apa.org/style-grammar-guidelines/bias-free-language/general-principles

08-26 https://translanguageprimer.com

08-27 https://assets.brand.ubc.ca/downloads/ubc_indigenous_peoples_language_guide.pdf

08-28 https://www.ingramspark.com/

08-29 https://www.lulu.com/

08-30 https://www.bookbaby.com/

08-31 https://kdp.amazon.com/en_US/

08-32 https://weshouldgettogether.com/designer-to-author

08-33 https://ijeomaoluo.substack.com/

08-34 https://onemorequestion.substack.com/

08-35 https://www.authorlearningcenter.com/publishing/distribution-sales/w/libraries/7658/how-to-get-your-book-into-public-libraries-and-why-it-matters

08-36 https://www.sidebarsaturdays.com/

08-37 https://docs.google.com/document/d/1GXJ3ixY9Vz5S9oiMXJqzQkoa-QOiptvLiZAuJyk_HtDo/edit

INDEX

ABOUT A BOOK APART

We cover the emerging and essential topics in web design and development with style, clarity, and above all, brevity—because working designer-developers can't afford to waste time.

COLOPHON

The text is set in FF Yoga and its companion, FF Yoga Sans, both by Xavier Dupré. Headlines and cover are set in Titling Gothic by David Berlow.

 This book was printed in the United States using FSC certified papers.